ALL OVER THE MAP AGAIN

Another Extraordinary Atlas of the United States

featuring towns that actually exist!

David Jouris

Ten Speed Press

Grateful acknowledgement is made for permission to reprint a portion of the lyrics from the following songs: "The Big Country" ©1976, 1977, 1978 Bleu Disque Music Co. / Index Music. Published by Index Music / Bleu Disque Music. All Rights Reserved. Used by Permission of the Publisher • "Chattanooga Choo-Choo" words & music by Harry Warren and Mack Gordon © 1941 (Renewed) Twentieth Century Music Corporation. All Rights controlled by EMI Feist Catalog Inc., All Rights Reserved. Used by Permission. Warner Bros. Publications U. S. Inc., Miami, FL 33014 • "Brilliant Mistake" (MacManus) ©1985 Plangent Visions Music Inc. (ASCAP). All Rights Reserved. Used by Permission. • Thank you.

 • Distributed in Australia by E. J. Dwyer Pty. Ltd., in Canada by Publishers Group West, in New Zealand by Tandem Press, in South Africa by Real Books, and in the United Kingdom and Europe by Airlift Books. • Cover design by David Jouris and Nancy Austin. Interior design and maps by David Jouris. • *Less Logic. More Magic.*

Library of Congress Cataloging-in-Publication Data: Jouris, David. All over the map again / by David Jouris. p. cm. ISBN 0-89815-835-4 1. Names, Geographical—United States—Maps. 2. United States—Humor—Maps. I. Title. G1200.J57 1996 [G&M] 912.73—dc20 96-12524 CIP MAP

First printing 1996. • Printed in Hong Kong. (The name is Cantonese for "fragrant harbor.")

A number of thematic maps similar to the ones in this atlas (on subjects such as animals, literature, optimism, and Christmas) appear in a recent series of black-and-white postcards produced by Hold the Mustard Productions at P.O. Box 822 Berkeley CA 94701 U.S.A. Catalog $1.

Ten Speed Press • Post Office Box 7123 • Berkeley, California 94707

1 2 3 4 5 6 7 8 9 10 — 02 01 00 99 98 97 96

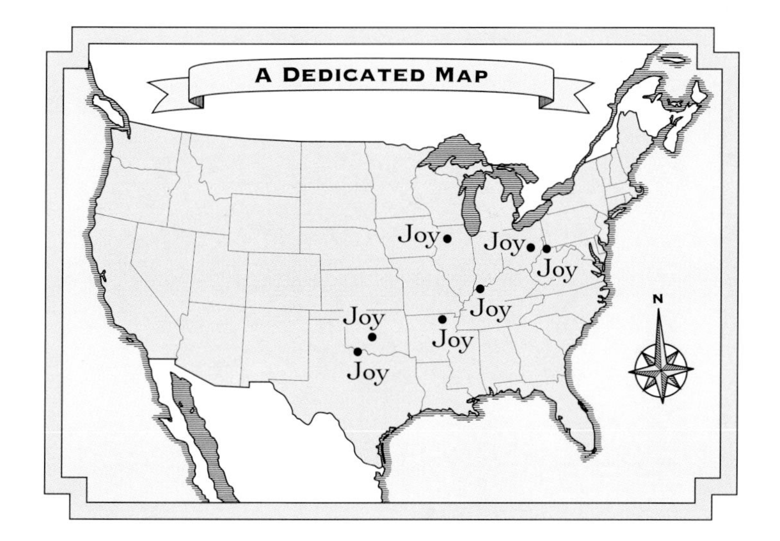

Joy seems to be a product of the geography.
—IAN FRAZIER

For Joy

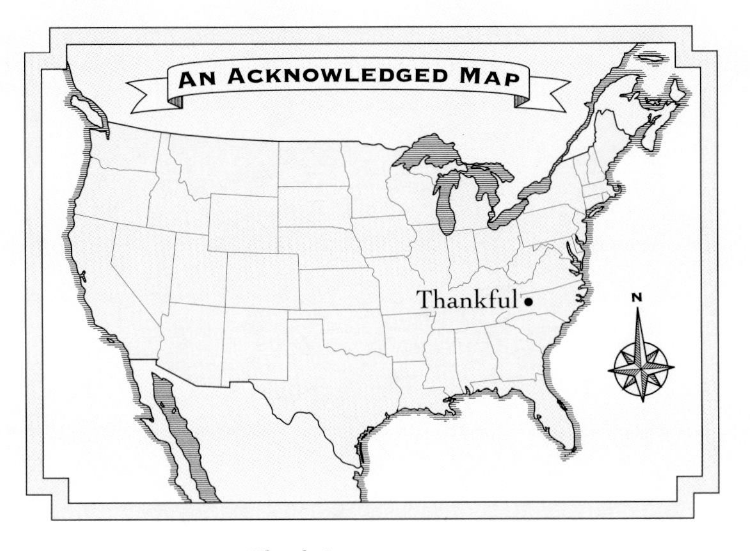

Thanks!
—Rudyard Kipling

Acknowledgments

For their Assistance, Enthusiasm, Inspiration, and Kindness: thanks to Sally Aberg, Linda Allison, James Barnes, Jeff Becom, Stephanie Berk, Lisa Martine Bernstein, Lilo Bloch, Liz & Richard Bordow, Janice Campbell, Linda Chester, Robin Chin, Judy & Tom Connell, Jennifer Lynn Connell, Laurie A. Fox, Max Greenstreet, John Grimes, Chuck & Karla Herndon, Kristen Hoehler, David & Laura Holstrom, Bill & Joanne Jouris, Donald & Virginia Jouris, Maira Kalman, John Kadyk, Virginia Kearns, Lazaris, David Loveall, Donna Latte, Jackie Leventhal, Lewis McArthur, Gunnar & Marcella Madsen, Allen McKinney, Kirsty Melville, D. Patrick Miller, Tim Miller, P. J. O'Brien, Patrick Ritter, Betsy & Ken Rock, Hebe Schafer, Dan X. Solo, George Stewart, Iaen Sullivan, Donna Tiffany, Todd Walton, Bill Wells, George Young, plus some wonderfully helpful private citizens, archivists, chambers of commerce, historical societies, post offices, town halls, and a trove of libraries and librarians—including the diverse libraries of the University of California (especially the Map Room, Doe Library, & Pacific Film Archive on the Berkeley campus), the Berkeley Public Library (especially Diane Davenport), and the staff of the Geography & Map Reading Room at the Library of Congress (especially Tanya Allison, Kathryn Engstrom, James Flatness, & Ronald Grim).

CONTENTS

N

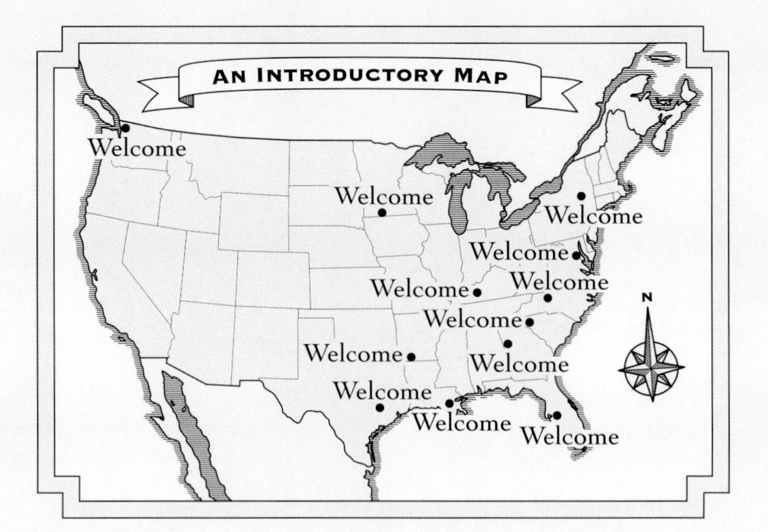

It is very difficult to say where a voyage begins.
First of course there must be a dream, a longing
for out-of-the-way places.
—**Peter Hamilton**

Introduction

The next time you hear someone claim there's no justice in this world, you can assure them that there is—and it's in West Virginia. It's just one of more than a hundred towns with names relating to the law on "A Strictly Legal Map." That thematic map and the thirty-three others presented here cover subjects as diverse as mathematics, Shakespeare, transportation, and cheese.

This atlas continues in the vein of my first book—*All Over the Map*. Working on that volume, I found myself coming up with many wonderful theme possibilities that I didn't have the space to include. This book presents those maps—and a number of other, more recent discoveries.

Two maps in this collection use slightly different formats than the others. "A Gone But Not Forgotten Map" shows former names of present-day towns. The names were changed over the years for a variety of reasons, but often the explanation was that the old name didn't sit well with the residents; if you lived in Skunk's Misery, you might have thought a change was in order, too. The citizens there changed the name several times—trying out Harrison, Slocum Hollow, Unionville, and Scrantonia—before settling down with the current name: Scranton, PA.

Occasionally, a proposed change wouldn't gain enough acceptance to alter the old name. Some residents of Hamilton, OH, didn't find their town's name to be particularly exciting; they began a movement to add some pizzazz by slightly altering it to "Hamilton!", but a majority of the populace just couldn't get keyed up about the change.

The other map with an unusual arrangement is "A Capital of the World Map." It consists of products or activities for which a town claims to be preeminent. These boasts aren't necessarily backed up with statistical proof, but do often have some basis in truth. It's not unusual, however, for more than one town to stake out the same claim. (The towns of Worthington, MN, and Cuero, TX, each year settle the question of which is the Turkey Capital of the World by staging a Turkey Race—the winning bird capturing the title for its hometown. (They apparently don't consult another claimant—Harrisonburg, PA.)

A question that comes to mind while one is immersed in the study of unusual place-names is just what to call the citizens of some of these towns. Should the residents of Villa, OH (on "An Architectural Map") be called Villains? Would one actually say the good citizens of Liberty, NE (on "A Patriotic Map") are Libertines? Are folks from Ideal, SD (on "A Utopian Map") properly called Idealists? And would those who live in Beehive, AL (on "An Armed & Dangerous Map") be called Bees? (Beehive, by the way, is a term for a type of explosive charge that is able to penetrate armor.)

Several matters of form may be of interest to the reader of this atlas. To begin with, not every town that could justifiably fit a theme actually made it onto the map, due to space limitations. Secondly, the terms "Native American" and "Indian" are used interchangeably in the text, following the example set by many current Native American writers. Lastly, should you be puzzled by any of the terms that appear on the maps in this atlas, a comprehensive dictionary can often provide enlightenment. In some cases, however, a deeper study of the particular theme may be called for. A journey to the library, perhaps with some assistance from a reference librarian, may prove especially helpful. Bon voyage.

I find mapmaking tremendously fun. It provides the excitement of travel, the pleasure of learning, and the joy of discovery. And anybody can do it because, as mapmakers like to point out, "Geography is everywhere."

David Jouris
Berkeley, Calif.
Spring 1996

The shorter and the plainer the better.
—BEATRIX POTTER

The following postal zip code abbreviations for the fifty states are used in this atlas:

AK	Alaska	LA	Louisiana	OH	Ohio
AL	Alabama	MA	Massachusetts	OK	Oklahoma
AR	Arkansas	MD	Maryland	OR	Oregon
AZ	Arizona	ME	Maine	PA	Pennsylvania
CA	California	MI	Michigan	RI	Rhode Island
CO	Colorado	MN	Minnesota	SC	South Carolina
CT	Connecticut	MO	Missouri	SD	South Dakota
DE	Delaware	MS	Mississippi	TN	Tennessee
FL	Florida	MT	Montana	TX	Texas
GA	Georgia	NB	Nebraska	UT	Utah
HI	Hawaii	NC	North Carolina	VT	Vermont
IA	Iowa	ND	North Dakota	VA	Virginia
ID	Idaho	NH	New Hampshire	WA	Washington
IL	Illinois	NJ	New Jersey	WI	Wisconsin
IN	Indiana	NM	New Mexico	WV	West Virginia
KS	Kansas	NV	Nevada	WY	Wyoming
K	Kentucky	NY	New York		

The smallest post office in the United States is located in Ochopee, FL (probably from a Seminole word meaning "hickory tree"). It occupies a tiny building with barely forty-two square feet of floor space—apparently enough to provide for the rural community it serves. The largest post office is the massive Chicago Main Post Office that is over three million square feet in size—more than twice as large as any other postal facility in the nation. The name Chicago is derived from an Algonquian word *Chigagou,* meaning "onion place."

And, by the way, zip code 90210 (in Beverly Hills, CA, of course) has the distinction of representing the richest per-capita area in the country.

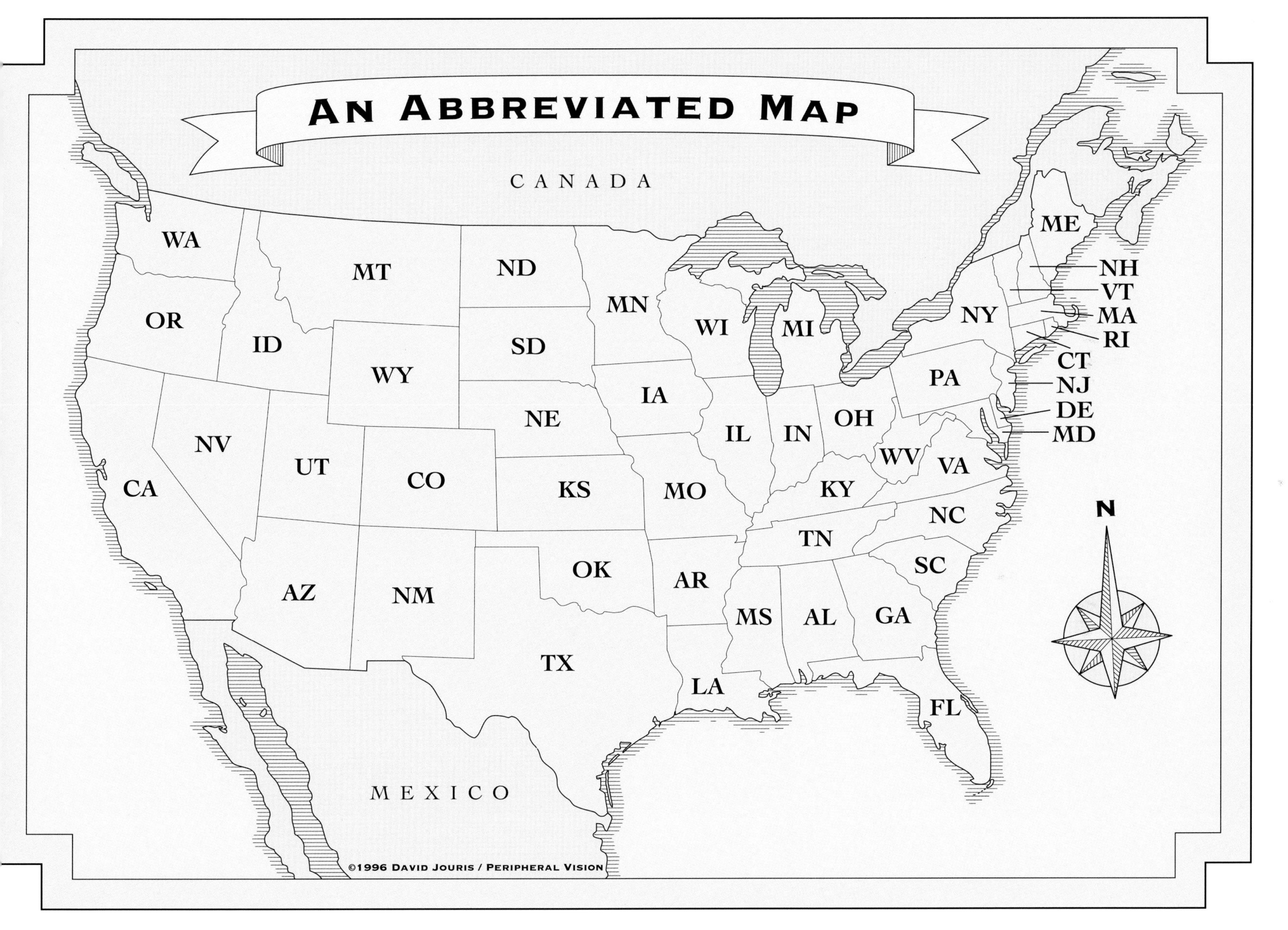
AN ABBREVIATED MAP
CANADA
WA
MT
ND
MN
ME
NH
VT
MA
RI
CT
NJ
DE
MD
OR
ID
WY
SD
WI
MI
NY
PA
IA
NE
IL
IN
OH
NV
UT
CO
KS
MO
WV
VA
KY
CA
NC
TN
OK
AR
SC
AZ
NM
MS
AL
GA
TX
LA
FL
N
MEXICO
©1996 DAVID JOURIS / PERIPHERAL VISION

Everybody has their own America.
—ANDY WARHOL

NOURISHING MAPS

Helping to Satisfy Your Hunger for Geography

I didn't squawk about the steak, dear. I merely said I didn't see that old horse that used to be tethered outside here.

—**W. C. Fields**, *to a waitress in the film "Never Give a Sucker an Even Break"*

Dinner in the diner, nothing could be finer
Than to have your ham 'n' eggs in Carolina.

—**Mack Gordon**, "Chattanooga Choo-Choo"

Located on Main Street in **Sandwich, IL**, is Paul's Diner—an authentic railroad dining car with a colorful history. It was built in 1893 for the World's Exhibition in Chicago; in the 1920s, Franklin Roosevelt used it when campaigning; since 1931 it has been a diner serving typical American fare. The Illinois town was named for **Sandwich, MA**, which in turn was named for Sandwich (*sand* "sandy soil" + *wic* "landing place"), in the English county of Kent. It was from England's fourth Earl of Sandwich, John Montagu, that the popular food name was taken. The Earl, notorious for his gambling, often lunched on meat between two slices of bread to avoid having to leave the poker table for nourishment.

Toast, NC, got its name back in 1927 when the community was looking for a more interesting name than the one it had—The Crossroad. One evening, the local school principal was shopping in the grocery store when "Toast" popped into his head. Accounts don't indicate whether the fellow was inspired while looking at bread—or bottles of liquor.

Jelly, CA, commemorates Andrew Jelly, who once operated a ferry across the Sacramento River at this location. And postmaster James A. Murphy used his initials to create the name for **Jam, MI**.

One delightful aspect of the world of diners, mostly gone from the scene today, was the playful lingo used by waitresses to communicate with short-order cooks. Terms like *Wreck a Pair* (signifying two scrambled eggs), *Adam and Eve on a Raft* (two eggs on toast), *Pig Between the Sheets* (ham sandwich), *Put Out the Lights and Cry* (liver and onions), *Noah's Boy with Murphy Carrying a Wreath* (ham and potatoes with cabbage), and *The Gentleman Will Take a Chance* (hash), lent a colorful flavor to otherwise ordinary fare. The soda fountain had its lingo too: *Black Cow* (chocolate soda with chocolate ice cream), *Chicago* (all-pineapple sundae), *Drag One Through Georgia* (Coca-Cola® with chocolate syrup), *Shake One in the Hay* (strawberry milkshake), and *Make it Cackle* (signaling the addition of a raw egg in the milkshake) were just a few of the expressions employed by soda jerks. And prior to World War II, there was an elaborate numerical code used by many restaurants. For example: *One* signaled a hamburger (*Twenty-One* was two hamburgers; *Thirty-One*, three hamburgers); *Forty-Four* stood for a cup of coffee; *Fifty-One* was a cup of hot chocolate; *Ninety-Six* meant a customer was leaving without paying. One remnant of this code is still used today: *Eighty-Six*—meaning "we're out of it" or "get rid of it."

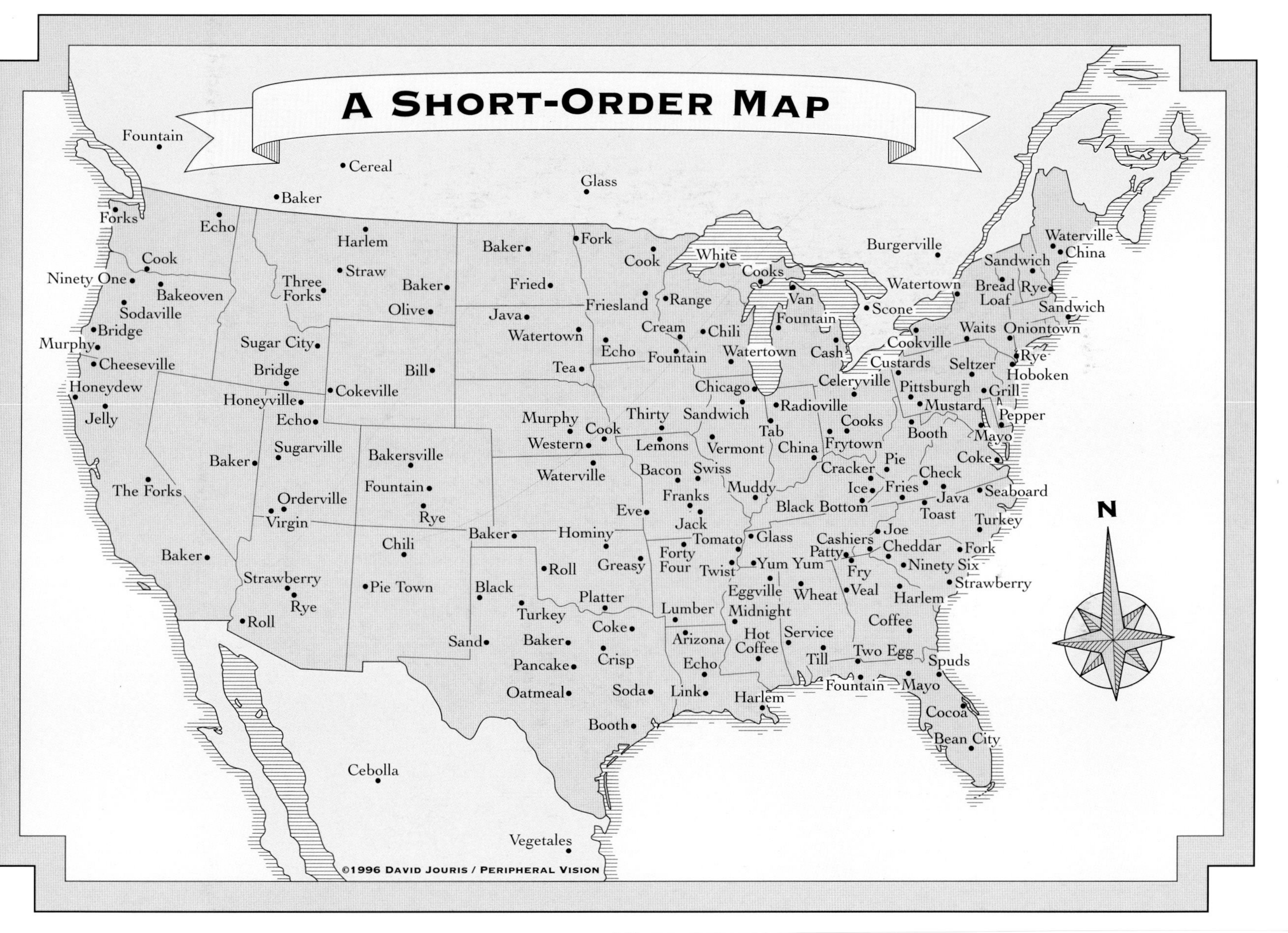
A SHORT-ORDER MAP
Fountain
Cereal
Baker
Glass
Forks
Echo
Harlem
Baker
Fork
Cook
White
Cooks
Burgerville
Waterville
China
Cook
Ninety One
Bakeoven
Three Forks
Straw
Baker
Fried
Friesland
Range
Van
Watertown
Sandwich
Bread Loaf
Rye
Sandwich
Sodaville
Olive
Java
Fountain
Scone
Bridge
Murphy
Sugar City
Watertown
Cream
Chili
Waits
Oniontown
Cookville
Echo
Fountain
Watertown
Cash
Rye
Cheeseville
Bridge
Bill
Tea
Custards
Seltzer
Hoboken
Honeydew
Cokeville
Chicago
Celeryville
Pittsburgh
Grill
Honeyville
Radioville
Mustard
Jelly
Echo
Murphy
Thirty
Sandwich
Cooks
Pepper
Cook
Tab
Booth
Mayo
Western
Lemons
Vermont
China
Frytown
Sugarville
Baker
Bakersville
Waterville
Bacon
Swiss
Cracker
Pie
Coke
Check
Muddy
Ice
Fries
Seaboard
The Forks
Fountain
Franks
Java
Orderville
Black Bottom
Toast
Eve
Virgin
Rye
Jack
Turkey
Baker
Hominy
Joe
Glass
Tomato
Cashiers
Chili
Cheddar
Fork
Patty
Baker
Forty Four
Greasy
Yum Yum
Ninety Six
Roll
Twist
Fry
Strawberry
Strawberry
Pie Town
Black
Eggville
Wheat
Veal
Rye
Platter
Harlem
Midnight
Lumber
Turkey
Roll
Coffee
Coke
Hot Coffee
Service
Arizona
Sand
Baker
Two Egg
Till
Crisp
Spuds
Echo
Pancake
Fountain
Mayo
Oatmeal
Soda
Link
Harlem
Cocoa
Booth
Bean City
Cebolla
Vegetales
N

There are two things that will be believed of any man whatsoever, and one of them is that he has taken to drink.
—**Booth Tarkington**

Water taken in moderation cannot hurt anybody.
—**Mark Twain**

During the California gold rush of 1849, **Whiskeytown, CA**, originated as the mining camp of Whiskey Creek, so called because a barrel of whiskey fell off a pack mule as it was crossing the creek. After a while, in what seemed to have been an attempt to change its image, the town had a series of less colorful names, such as Blair. Finally, in the 1950s, the town put the alcohol content back into its name. Apparently not wishing to give the appearance of being obsessed with liquids, the citizenry opted to drop *Creek* in favor of *-town*.

The town of **Tea, SD**, had previously been named Byron; but before being authorized to open a post office, it was forced to change its name since there was already another town in the state with that name. A number of the residents were ardent supporters of the name *Beer*, after their beverage of choice. Their suggestion, however, was turned down as it was thought that unfavorable publicity might result. Apparently, by mid afternoon, after spending a number of hours trying to reach consensus, someone realized that it was "time for tea"—and Tea it was.

When residents of the rural community of **Punch, TN**, started submitting town name possibilites to the postal authorities, the only response seemed to be, "That name is already in use." This went on for some time until John Carter, one of the first merchants there, submitted the names *Punch* and *Judy*, since these puppet characters were very popular at the time. The name Judy was "already in use;" but the other name was available and, thus, a postal route was set up to serve Punch.

At it turns out, the name of **Smoky, VA**, has no relation to the smoky characteristic of an alcoholic beverage. The previous name of this rural community was Smoky Ordinary. (In colonial times, it was the location of a tavern, or "ordinary," where meals were served.) During the American Revolution, British troops burned down the ordinary, bringing about the descriptive name. As time went by, however, the *Ordinary* part of the name also went up in smoke.

In 1850 settlers in a swampy part of southern Florida named their river the Corkscrew for its many twists and turns. The community of **Corkscrew, FL**, took its name from the river, although the river has since been renamed the Imperial.

That concoction of whiskey and sweet vermouth with a maraschino cherry, known as the Manhattan cocktail, was named for the New York borough where it was first made. Its originator, a New York socialite named Jennie Jerome, is better known for a later creation—she was Winston Churchill's mother.

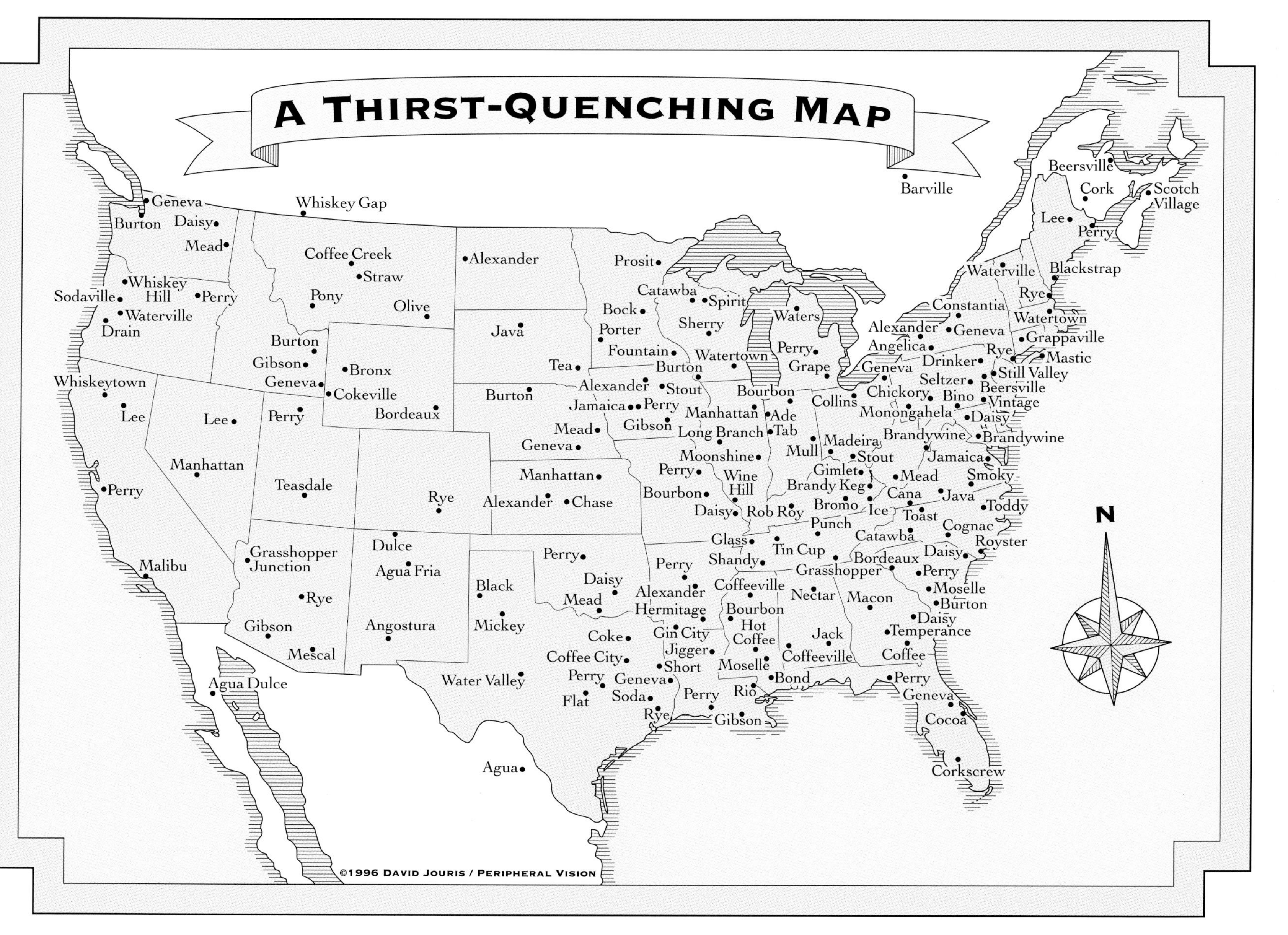
A THIRST-QUENCHING MAP
Beersville
Barville
Cork
Scotch Village
Lee
Perry
Geneva
Whiskey Gap
Burton
Daisy
Mead
Coffee Creek
Straw
Alexander
Prosit
Waterville
Blackstrap
Whiskey Hill
Sodaville
Perry
Waterville
Drain
Pony
Olive
Catawba
Spirit
Rye
Constantia
Bock
Sherry
Waters
Watertown
Java
Porter
Alexander
Geneva
Grappaville
Burton
Fountain
Watertown
Perry
Angelica
Rye
Mastic
Gibson
Bronx
Tea
Burton
Grape
Geneva
Drinker
Still Valley
Geneva
Alexander
Seltzer
Beersville
Whiskeytown
Cokeville
Burton
Stout
Bourbon
Collins
Chickory
Bino
Vintage
Jamaica
Perry
Manhattan
Ade
Monongahela
Daisy
Lee
Lee
Perry
Bordeaux
Mead
Gibson
Long Branch
Tab
Madeira
Brandywine
Brandywine
Geneva
Mull
Stout
Jamaica
Moonshine
Manhattan
Perry
Gimlet
Mead
Smoky
Wine Hill
Brandy Keg
Cana
Java
Teasdale
Rye
Alexander
Chase
Bourbon
Bromo
Toddy
Perry
Daisy
Rob Roy
Ice
Toast
Punch
Cognac
Glass
Catawba
Royster
Dulce
Tin Cup
Daisy
Grasshopper Junction
Perry
Shandy
Bordeaux
Agua Fria
Perry
Grasshopper
Perry
Malibu
Daisy
Coffeeville
Black
Alexander
Moselle
Rye
Mead
Nectar
Macon
Burton
Hermitage
Bourbon
Daisy
Gibson
Angostura
Mickey
Hot Coffee
Temperance
Coke
Gin City
Jack
Mescal
Jigger
Coffee City
Coffeeville
Coffee
Short
Moselle
Agua Dulce
Water Valley
Perry
Geneva
Bond
Perry
Rio
Flat
Soda
Perry
Geneva
Rye
Gibson
Cocoa
Agua
Corkscrew
N
©1996 DAVID JOURIS / PERIPHERAL VISION

Poets have been mysteriously silent on the subject of cheese.
—G. K. CHESTERTON

It is stretching things to call **Cheeseville, CA**, a town, as the entire place is now on a ranch and only ruins remain of the original cheese factory from which it takes its name. In former times, a small business community grew up around a dairy located here, including a creamery and a blacksmith shop. The creamery was used by all of the local farms, and cheese was sold to people far and wide, including the men who were mining gold in the region. The factory itself lasted for about thirty years, from the 1880s until its demise early in the 1900s, but the place is still referred to as Cheeseville.

Tillamook, OR, was named for a tribe of Salish Indians who lived in the region. Commercial cheesemaking began here in the 1890s, and the name Tillamook is now a trademarked type of cheddar cheese. Are the cheesemakers passing up a golden opportunity by not making a gooey brie of some sort—and naming it *Runamook*?

In the 1870s, Gardner Colby, a Boston financier, helped raise money for a railroad line to a region in central Wisconsin, and, thus, the village of **Colby, WI**, is named for him. A few years later, a cheesemaker named Joseph Steinwand invented the process for a new type of cheese that he named Colby, after the town. It is quite possible that Steinwand simply made the mistake of adding too much water while making cheddar, thus producing a softer, cheddarlike cheese that proved to be quite popular.

Cheesequake, NJ, isn't named for an unsteady dessert, as some have suggested, but rather derives from a Native American word, *chauquisitt*, meaning "upland."

The word "yankee" may actually be derived from the name *Jan Kees*—a Dutch version of John Doe. In the mid seventeenth century, the Dutch territory of New York was traded to the British in exchange for Surinam. Although the Dutch language continued to be spoken in New York by large numbers of residents, the British referred to the Dutch with the derogatory term *Jan Kees*. The term translates as "John Cheese"—an acknowledgment of the Dutch love of this dairy product. Over time the spelling of the name changed so the English spelling would approximate the Dutch pronounciation.

Any discussion of cheese names ought not to be concluded without at least a mention of Essex, described by one expert as "a fabled English cheese so unappealing, they say, that it caused dogs to bark."

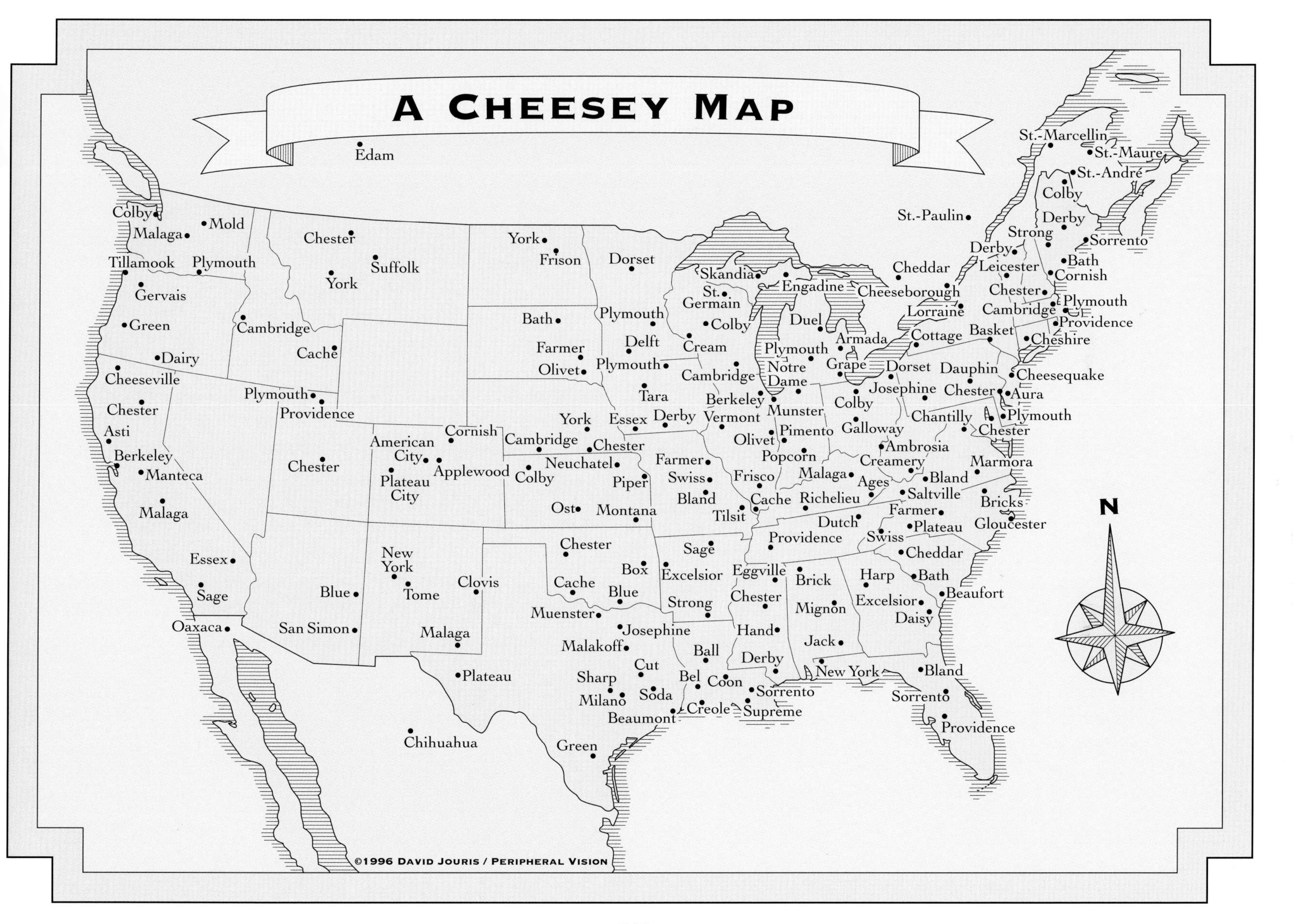
A CHEESEY MAP
Edam
St.-Marcellin
St.-Maure
St.-André
Colby
St.-Paulin
Derby
Strong
Sorrento
Colby
Mold
Malaga
Chester
York
Frison
Derby
Bath
Tillamook
Plymouth
Suffolk
Dorset
Skandia
Cheddar
Leicester
Cornish
York
St. Germain
Engadine
Cheeseborough
Chester
Plymouth
Gervais
Plymouth
Cambridge
Lorraine
Providence
Green
Cambridge
Bath
Colby
Duel
Cottage
Basket
Cheshire
Cache
Farmer
Delft
Cream
Armada
Plymouth
Dairy
Olivet
Plymouth
Grape
Notre Dame
Dorset
Dauphin
Cheesequake
Cheeseville
Cambridge
Josephine
Chester
Aura
Plymouth
Tara
Berkeley
Colby
Chester
Providence
York
Essex
Derby
Vermont
Munster
Chantilly
Plymouth
Asti
Cornish
Pimento
Galloway
Chester
American City
Cambridge
Chester
Olivet
Ambrosia
Berkeley
Applewood
Neuchatel
Popcorn
Manteca
Chester
Farmer
Creamery
Marmora
Plateau City
Colby
Piper
Swiss
Frisco
Malaga
Bland
Ages
Bland
Cache
Richelieu
Saltville
Bricks
Malaga
Ost
Montana
Tilsit
Farmer
Dutch
Plateau
Gloucester
Swiss
Chester
Providence
Sage
Cheddar
New York
Essex
Box
Excelsior
Eggville
Brick
Harp
Bath
Sage
Blue
Tome
Clovis
Cache
Blue
Strong
Chester
Beaufort
Excelsior
Mignon
Daisy
Muenster
Oaxaca
San Simon
Malaga
Josephine
Hand
Malakoff
Jack
Ball
Derby
Cut
New York
Bland
Plateau
Sharp
Bel
Coon
Sorrento
Sorrento
Milano
Soda
Creole
Supreme
Beaumont
Providence
Chihuahua
Green
N
©1996 DAVID JOURIS / PERIPHERAL VISION

N

ECCENTRIC MAPS

More Strangers in a Strange Land

There is nothing permanent except change.
—HERACLITUS

Present-day names:

1 - Auburn, WA
2 - Lebam, WA
3 - Latah, WA
4 - Marshland, OR
5 - Needy, OR
6 - Twickenham, OR
7 - Drewsy, OR
8 - Azalea, OR
9 - Grenada, CA
10 - Johnstonville, CA
11 - North Bloomfield, CA
12 - Ione, CA
13 - El Cerrito, CA
14 - San Francisco, CA
15 - Hopeton, CA
16 - Ivanhoe, CA
17 - Cambria, CA
18 - Kernville, CA
19 - Barstow, CA
20 - Fawnskin, CA
21 - Caliente, NV
22 - Tonopah, NV
23 - Yerington, NV
24 - Wadsworth, NV
25 - Jiggs, NV
26 - Burley, ID
27 - Soda Springs, ID
28 - Payette, ID
29 - Moscow, ID
30 - Florence, MT
31 - Helena, MT
32 - Anaconda, MT
33 - Bannack, MT
34 - Arvada, WY
35 - Emblem, WY
36 - Smoot, WY
37 - Wamsutter, WY
38 - Lewiston, UT
39 - Fairfield, UT
40 - Antimony, UT
41 - Happy Jack, AZ
42 - Lowell, AZ
43 - White City, NM
44 - Arenas Valley, NM
45 - Lingo, NM
46 - Continental Divide, NM
47 - Rainsville, NM
48 - Capulin, NM
49 - Oxford, CO
50 - Thatcher, CO
51 - Molina, CO
52 - Leadville, CO
53 - Joes, CO
54 - Broomfield, CO
55 - Mascot, NE
56 - Carleton, NE
57 - Glenvil, NE
58 - Royal, NE
59 - Eli, NE
60 - Dante, SD
61 - Parmelee, SD
62 - Marvin, SD
63 - Menoken, ND
64 - Mandan, ND
65 - Big Falls, MN
66 - Cuyuna, MN
67 - Winona, MN
68 - Granada, MN
69 - Williamstown, IA
70 - Keokuk, IA
71 - Leonardville, KS
72 - Dodge City, KS
73 - Hackney, KS
74 - Bernice, OK
75 - Taft, OK
76 - Bessie, OK
77 - Blair, OK
78 - Coleman, OK
79 - Alanreed, TX
80 - Tell, TX
81 - Peerless, TX
82 - Big Spring, TX
83 - El Paso, TX
84 - Rockwood, TX
85 - Ariola, TX
86 - Buda, TX
87 - Langtry, TX
88 - Edna, TX
89 - Tilden, TX
90 - Alamo, TX
91 - Supreme, LA
92 - Sulphur, LA
93 - Bethany, LA
94 - Wesley Chapel, AR
95 - Cash, AR
96 - Fagus, MO
97 - Nevada, MO
98 - Cedar Grove, IL
99 - Oblong, IL
100 - Mildred, IL
101 - Lambert, IL
102 - Hazel Green, WI
103 - Johnsonville, WI
104 - Calumet, MI
105 - Trombly, MI
106 - Keystone, MI
107 - North Bradley, MI
108 - Wyoming, MI
109 - Howardsville, MI
110 - Bringhurst, IN
111 - Redkey, IN
112 - Octavia, KY
113 - Welchs Creek, KY
114 - Savoyard, KY
115 - Memphis, TN
116 - Rexford, MS
117 - DeLisle, MS
118 - Oxford, AL
119 - Fredonia, AL
120 - Victoria, AL
121 - Sunrise, FL
122 - St. Catherine, FL
123 - Gainesville, FL
124 - Melrose, FL
125 - Milton, FL
126 - Adel, GA
127 - Weston, GA
128 - Atlanta, GA
129 - Montmorenci, SC
130 - Prosperity, SC
131 - Liberty, SC
132 - Friendship, NC
133 - Aurora, NC
134 - Cedarrock, NC
135 - Haynesville, VA
136 - Stony Bottom, WV
137 - Mountain, WV
138 - Shady Glen, OH
139 - Scranton, PA
140 - Lake Lynn, PA
141 - Madison, MD
142 - Frederica, DE
143 - Stanton, DE
144 - Lanoka Harbor, NJ
145 - New York, NY
146 - Ossining, NY
147 - Salamanca, NY
148 - Brookfield, NY
149 - Kingston, RI
150 - Pascoag, RI
151 - Boston, MA
152 - Conway, NH
153 - Portland, ME
154 - Augusta, ME
155 - Apohaqui, *Canada*
156 - Penobsquis, *Canada*
157 - Shinnickburn, *Canada*
158 - Ottawa, *Canada*
159 - Kenora, *Canada*
160 - Harding, *Canada*
161 - New Denver, *Canada*
162 - North Vancouver, *Canada*
163 - Hermosillo, *Mexico*
164 - Ciudad Obregón, *Mexico*
165 - Aquiles Serdán, *Mexico*

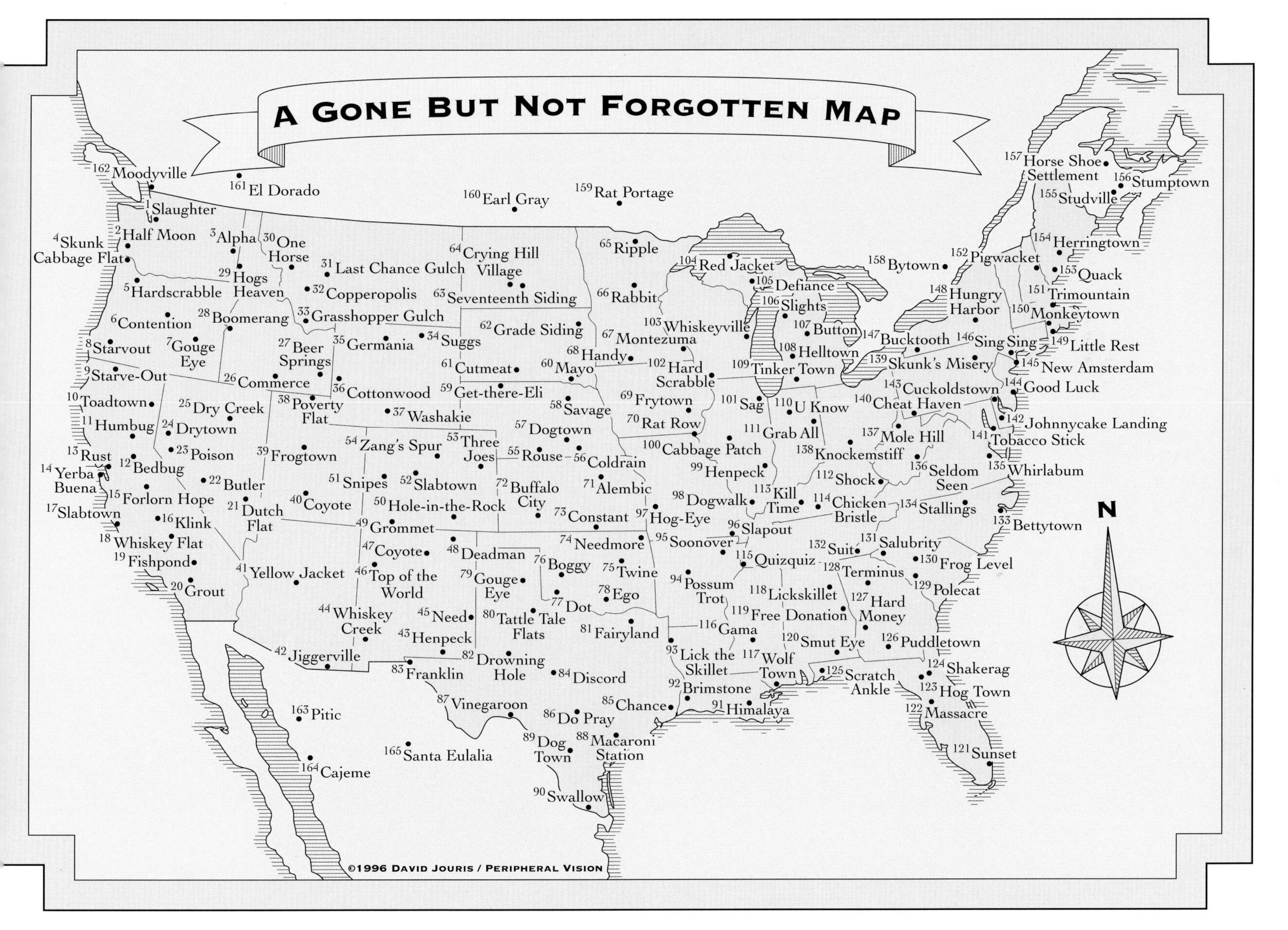
A Gone But Not Forgotten Map
1 Slaughter
2 Half Moon
3 Alpha
4 Skunk Cabbage Flat
5 Hardscrabble
6 Contention
7 Gouge Eye
8 Starvout
9 Starve-Out
10 Toadtown
11 Humbug
12 Bedbug
13 Rust
14 Yerba Buena
15 Forlorn Hope
16 Klink
17 Slabtown
18 Whiskey Flat
19 Fishpond
20 Grout
21 Dutch Flat
22 Butler
23 Poison
24 Drytown
25 Dry Creek
26 Commerce
27 Beer Springs
28 Boomerang
29 Hogs Heaven
30 One Horse
31 Last Chance Gulch
32 Copperopolis
33 Grasshopper Gulch
34 Suggs
35 Germania
36 Cottonwood
37 Washakie
38 Poverty Flat
39 Frogtown
40 Coyote
41 Yellow Jacket
42 Jiggerville
43 Henpeck
44 Whiskey Creek
45 Need
46 Top of the World
47 Coyote
48 Deadman
49 Grommet
50 Hole-in-the-Rock
51 Snipes
52 Slabtown
53 Three Joes
54 Zang's Spur
55 Rouse
56 Coldrain
57 Dogtown
58 Savage
59 Get-there-Eli
60 Mayo
61 Cutmeat
62 Grade Siding
63 Seventeenth Siding
64 Crying Hill Village
65 Ripple
66 Rabbit
67 Montezuma
68 Handy
69 Frytown
70 Rat Row
71 Alembic
72 Buffalo City
73 Constant
74 Needmore
75 Twine
76 Boggy
77 Dot
78 Ego
79 Gouge Eye
80 Tattle Tale Flats
81 Fairyland
82 Drowning Hole
83 Franklin
84 Discord
85 Chance
86 Do Pray
87 Vinegaroon
88 Macaroni Station
89 Dog Town
90 Swallow
91 Himalaya
92 Brimstone
93 Lick the Skillet
94 Possum Trot
95 Soonover
96 Slapout
97 Hog-Eye
98 Dogwalk
99 Henpeck
100 Cabbage Patch
101 Sag
102 Hard Scrabble
103 Whiskeyville
104 Red Jacket
105 Defiance
106 Slights
107 Button
108 Helltown
109 Tinker Town
110 U Know
111 Grab All
112 Shock
113 Kill Time
114 Chicken Bristle
115 Quizquiz
116 Gama
117 Wolf Town
118 Lickskillet
119 Free Donation
120 Smut Eye
121 Sunset
122 Massacre
123 Hog Town
124 Shakerag
125 Scratch Ankle
126 Puddletown
127 Hard Money
128 Terminus
129 Polecat
130 Frog Level
131 Salubrity
132 Suit
133 Bettytown
134 Stallings
135 Whirlabum
136 Seldom Seen
137 Mole Hill
138 Knockemstiff
139 Skunk's Misery
140 Cheat Haven
141 Tobacco Stick
142 Johnnycake Landing
143 Cuckoldstown
144 Good Luck
145 New Amsterdam
146 Sing Sing
147 Bucktooth
148 Hungry Harbor
149 Little Rest
150 Monkeytown
151 Trimountain
152 Pigwacket
153 Quack
154 Herringtown
155 Studville
156 Stumptown
157 Horse Shoe Settlement
158 Bytown
159 Rat Portage
160 Earl Gray
161 El Dorado
162 Moodyville
163 Pitic
164 Cajeme
165 Santa Eulalia
N
©1996 David Jouris / Peripheral Vision

It does not require many words to speak the truth.
—Chief Joseph

To be brief is almost a condition of being inspired.
—George Santayana

Most folks probably assume that since the community of **Brief, WA**, is very small, the name came from the fact that when you drive through it, your time there is brief. The truth is, the name originated in the early 1900s when the locals held a number of meetings to try to choose a name for their town. At one point, aggravated at the prospect of having to endure yet another lengthy meeting, one resident named Hettie Martin stood up and declared, "I don't care what you call it, but let's make it brief." Obviously, her fellow residents agreed.

There is a fine little story that explains how **Ink, AR**, came by its name. Supposedly the postal authorities approved the location for a post office and asked a local schoolteacher to get input from the residents on a possible name. The teacher sent a note to the parents of all her students explaining the search for a town name. Because she felt pencil might be hard to read, she included the instruction, "Write in ink."

The name of the rural community of **Ka, VA**, comes from the configuration of the roads that intersect there. From Ka (pronounced "Kay"), roads go in four different directions—to High Knob, Fort Blackmore, Duffield, and Dungannon—so that they look like the 11th letter of the alphabet.

Tax, GA, got its name because the post office was inside a mercantile store and it was there that county tax officials picked up local tax returns. With only three letters, the town name is brief—it's only in common usage that "tax" seems to go on forever.

Leander Blankenship, the first postmaster of a small village in West Virginia, was mulling over what to call the new post office one day in the early 1900s. While so occupied, a neighbor brought him a pie—and thus **Pie, WV**, came to be.

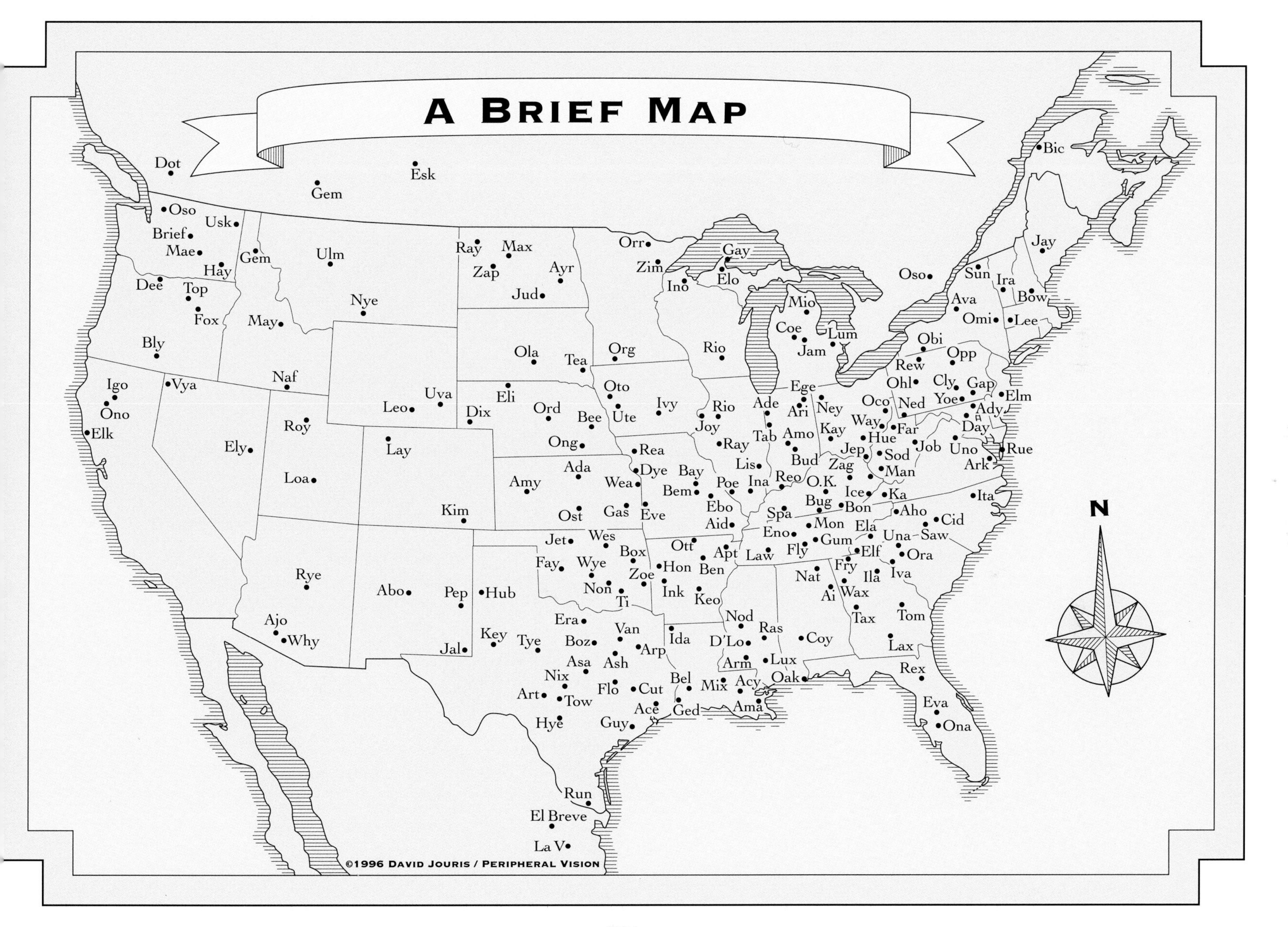
A BRIEF MAP
Dot
Esk
Gem
Oso
Usk
Brief
Mae
Hay
Gem
Ulm
Ray
Max
Zap
Ayr
Jud
Orr
Zim
Gay
Elo
Ino
Dee
Top
Fox
May
Nye
Bly
Oso
Sun
Ira
Jay
Bow
Ava
Omi
Lee
Bic
Mio
Coe
Lum
Jam
Rio
Ola
Tea
Org
Obi
Opp
Rew
Igo
Ono
Vya
Naf
Leo
Uva
Eli
Dix
Ord
Bee
Oto
Ute
Ivy
Rio
Joy
Ade
Tab
Ege
Ari
Ney
Oco
Ned
Ohl
Cly
Gap
Yoe
Elm
Ady
Day
Elk
Roy
Ely
Lay
Ong
Rea
Ray
Amo
Kay
Way
Hue
Far
Job
Uno
Rue
Jep
Sod
Ark
Loa
Ada
Dye
Bay
Lis
Bud
Zag
Man
Amy
Wea
Bem
Poe
Ina
Reo
O.K.
Ice
Ka
Ita
Kim
Ost
Gas
Eve
Ebo
Aid
Bug
Bon
Spa
Mon
Aho
Cid
Eno
Ela
Una
Saw
Jet
Wes
Box
Ott
Apt
Law
Fly
Gum
Elf
Ora
Fay
Wye
Hon
Ben
Fry
Iva
Ila
Zoe
Nat
Non
Ti
Ink
Keo
Ai
Wax
Rye
Abo
Pep
Hub
Era
Nod
Tax
Tom
Ajo
Why
Key
Tye
Boz
Van
Arp
Ida
D'Lo
Ras
Coy
Lax
Jal
Asa
Ash
Arm
Lux
Rex
Nix
Bel
Mix
Acy
Oak
Art
Tow
Flo
Cut
Ace
Ged
Ama
Eva
Ona
Hye
Guy
Run
El Breve
La V
N
©1996 DAVID JOURIS / PERIPHERAL VISION

It was a kind of dyslexia . . . a geographic dyslexia.
—ANNE TYLER

The town of **Reklaw, TX**, was named for Margaret Walker, who owned the land the town was built on. Since another post office already existed at that time with the name Walker, the citizens just reversed the letters. Only a few miles away from Reklaw is the town of **Sacul, TX**, named for an early settler, John Lucas. When Lucas's proper name was rejected by the postal authorities, its letters were also reversed.

The name of **Lebam, WA**, was created by a citizen who reversed the spelling of his daughter's name. The town had been called Half Moon, but apparently the Post Office Department in Washington, D.C., was going through one of its phases of objecting to two-word names and asked for a change. (The postal authorities also have periodic episodes of disliking alternate spellings of town names (insisting on "burg" rather than "burgh" and "boro" rather than "borough") or any name with an apostrophe (insisting on "Manns Choice, PA," rather than "Mann's Choice, PA," for example).

Glenelg, MD, is named for the estate Glenelg Manor, built by Joseph Tyson in the mid 1800s. The house features a facade modeled after an old castle in Scotland. Glenelg, Scotland, (from *gleann* "glen" + *elg* "Ireland") was an early immigration point for the Irish coming to the Highlands.

The town of Pekin became **Nikep, MD**, because there is a town named Pekin in Indiana. In the days before zip codes there was much misdelivered mail; when people wrote the address in script and abbreviated the state name, the "Md." looked too much like "Ind."

Levan, UT, appears to be a reversal of the word navel—and can it only be a coincidence that the town is located in the center of the state? Well, it's something to contemplate.

Some names at first glance do not seem to be reversed. For example: **Wabasso, FL**, is held to be a reversal from Ossabaw Island, GA. And the inclusion of a handfull of towns on this map suddenly becomes clear when the zip code abbreviation is included: **Lis, IL**; **Omaha, MO**; **Roy, OR**; and **Apollo, PA**.

Yreka, CA, was once the home of the ingeniously named Yreka Bakery, but alas, no longer; after a hundred years of service, the original bakery closed in the 1960s. An art gallery took over the location and, with a somewhat awkward nod to tradition, called itself the Yrella Gallery, a name as reversible as its predecessor.

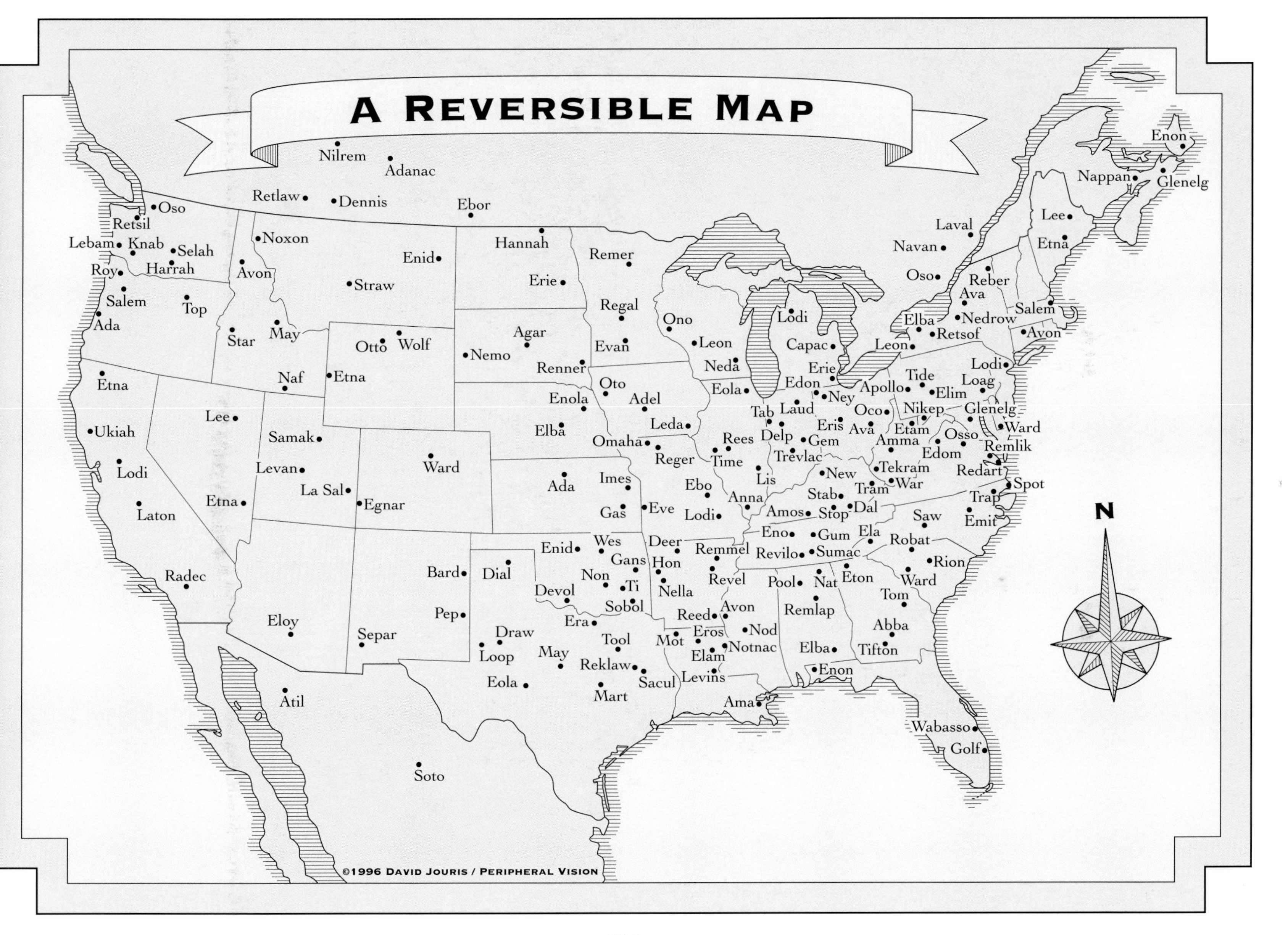
A REVERSIBLE MAP
Enon
Nilrem
Adanac
Nappan
Glenelg
Retlaw
Dennis
Oso
Ebor
Retsil
Lee
Laval
Lebam
Knab
Selah
Noxon
Hannah
Etna
Navan
Remer
Enid
Roy
Harrah
Avon
Straw
Erie
Oso
Reber
Salem
Top
Regal
Ava
Salem
Ono
Lodi
Elba
Nedrow
Ada
Star
May
Agar
Retsof
Avon
Otto
Wolf
Nemo
Leon
Capac
Leon
Evan
Neda
Renner
Lodi
Erie
Tide
Naf
Etna
Oto
Etna
Edon
Apollo
Loag
Eola
Elim
Enola
Adel
Ney
Tab
Laud
Oco
Nikep
Glenelg
Lee
Leda
Eris
Ava
Etam
Ward
Elba
Ukiah
Samak
Delp
Gem
Amma
Osso
Omaha
Rees
Remlik
Reger
Time
Trevlac
Edom
Ward
Levan
Lodi
Tekram
Redart
New
Ada
Imes
Ebo
Lis
War
Tram
Spot
Stab
Anna
La Sal
Egnar
Etna
Gas
Eve
Lodi
Amos
Stop
Dal
Trap
Laton
Saw
Emit
N
Eno
Gum
Ela
Wes
Deer
Robat
Enid
Remmel
Revilo
Sumac
Gans
Hon
Rion
Bard
Dial
Non
Revel
Eton
Radec
Ti
Pool
Nat
Ward
Devol
Nella
Tom
Sobol
Avon
Remlap
Pep
Reed
Eloy
Era
Nod
Abba
Draw
Separ
Eros
Tool
Mot
Notnac
Elba
Tifton
Loop
May
Elam
Reklaw
Enon
Levins
Eola
Sacul
Mart
Atil
Ama
Wabasso
Golf
Soto
©1996 DAVID JOURIS / PERIPHERAL VISION

Suppose you were an idiot. And suppose you were
a member of Congress. But I repeat myself.
—MARK TWAIN

It was déjà vu all over again.
—YOGI BERRA

Twinsburg, OH, is named for identical twins Moses and Aaron Wilcox, who bought land in this area and opened a general store in 1812. Not only did they look the same, but they married women who were sisters, each had the same number of children, and later both caught the same disease and died on the same day. And, as a final touch, they were buried in the same grave. Since 1976, Twinsburg has put on a festival that draws sets of twins from all over the world—running the gamut from those only a few months old to those well into their eighties.

It is usually said that **KoKo, TN**, got its name from the brand name of a candy bar that was on sale in the general store where mail was picked up by local residents. This may well be so, but the residents of KoKo, Yum Yum, and Nankipoo—all within a few dozen miles of each other in Tennessee—may be in for "a short, sharp shock" to learn that all three of these names are characters in Gilbert & Sullivan's light opera *The Mikado*.

James Eaton, postmaster and prominent merchant in a nearby town, first proposed that the rural residents secure a post office of their own in what is now **Soso, MS**. Eaton was known for responding to any question about his health or how his business was doing with the phrase "so so." When choosing a name for their new post office, the local farmers felt Eaton's phrase described their own feelings about life in the community.

Echo, MN, got its name in the late 1800s when the residents met several times to choose a name. Each time they selected one, it was rejected by the authorities because the citizens somehow managed to choose names that had already been given to other towns in the state. Finally, one frustrated resident suggested that since the names kept coming back to them, they might as well call the town Echo. **Echo, PA**, on the other hand, is named due to a number of ravines in the area that cause sounds to repeat.

It seems fair enough to list the town of Okay on the repetitive map because its mailing address is **Okay, OK**. Of course, it would only take a small adjustment to include cities and states such as New York, New York, but one has to draw the line somewhere.

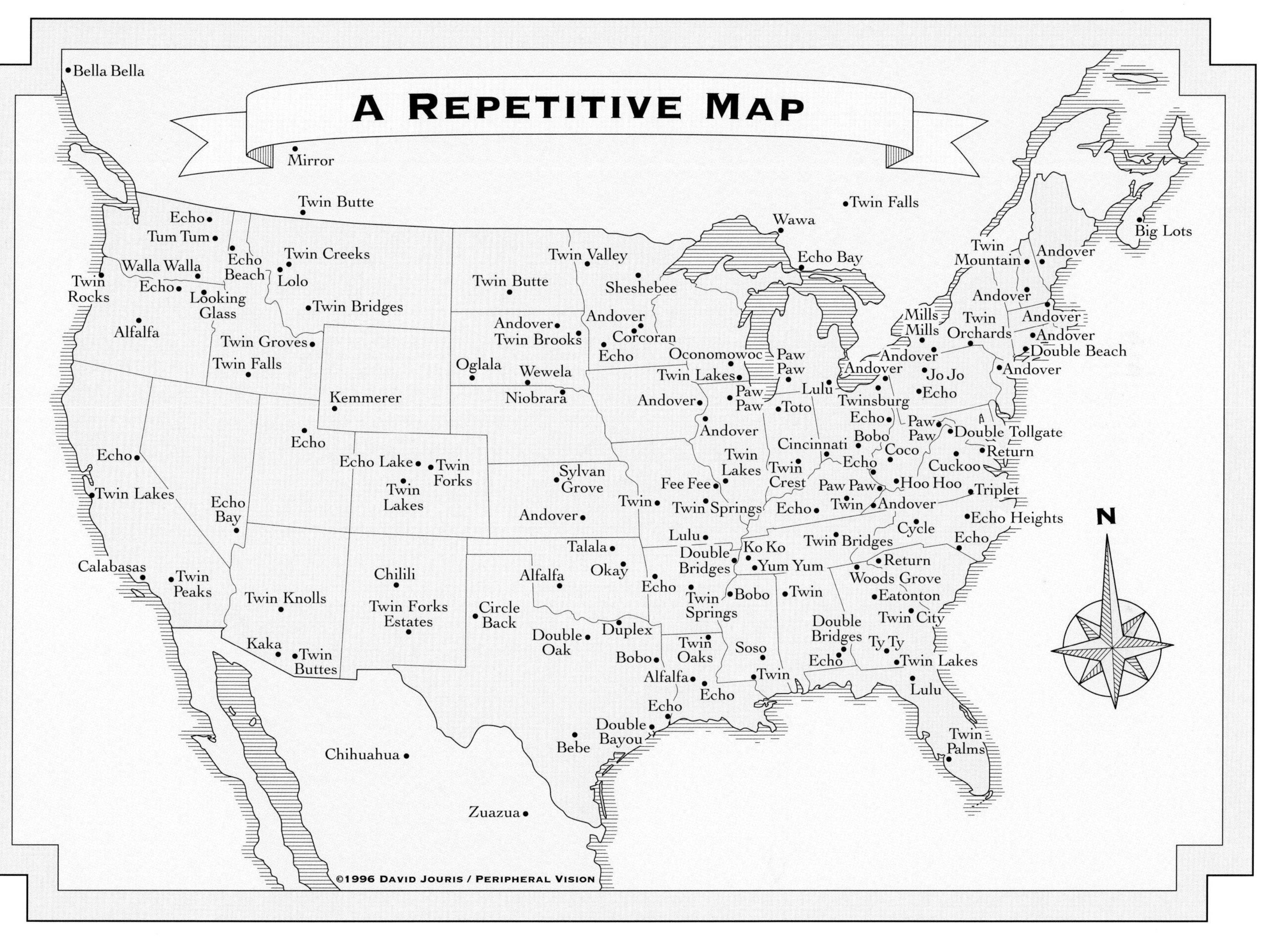
A REPETITIVE MAP
Bella Bella
Mirror
Twin Butte
Twin Falls
Wawa
Big Lots
Echo
Tum Tum
Echo Beach
Twin Creeks
Lolo
Walla Walla
Twin Rocks
Echo
Looking Glass
Twin Bridges
Alfalfa
Twin Groves
Twin Falls
Twin Valley
Sheshebee
Echo Bay
Twin Mountain
Andover
Twin Butte
Andover
Andover
Twin Brooks
Andover
Corcoran
Echo
Oconomowoc
Paw Paw
Mills Mills
Twin Orchards
Andover
Andover
Double Beach
Andover
Oglala
Wewela
Twin Lakes
Andover
Jo Jo
Andover
Niobrara
Andover
Paw Paw
Toto
Lulu
Twinsburg
Echo
Kemmerer
Andover
Echo
Bobo
Paw Paw
Double Tollgate
Echo
Cincinnati
Coco
Return
Echo Lake
Twin Forks
Twin Lakes
Twin Crest
Echo
Cuckoo
Sylvan Grove
Fee Fee
Paw Paw
Hoo Hoo
Echo
Twin Lakes
Twin Lakes
Echo Bay
Twin
Twin Springs
Echo
Twin
Andover
Triplet
Andover
Cycle
Echo Heights
Lulu
Twin Bridges
Echo
Talala
Double Bridges
Ko Ko
Yum Yum
Return
Woods Grove
Calabasas
Twin Peaks
Chilili
Okay
Alfalfa
Echo
Twin Knolls
Twin Springs
Bobo
Twin
Eatonton
Twin Forks Estates
Circle Back
Twin City
Duplex
Double Oak
Double Bridges
Kaka
Twin Buttes
Bobo
Twin Oaks
Soso
Ty Ty
Echo
Twin Lakes
Alfalfa
Twin
Echo
Lulu
Echo
Double Bayou
Bebe
Twin Palms
Chihuahua
Zuazua
N
©1996 DAVID JOURIS / PERIPHERAL VISION

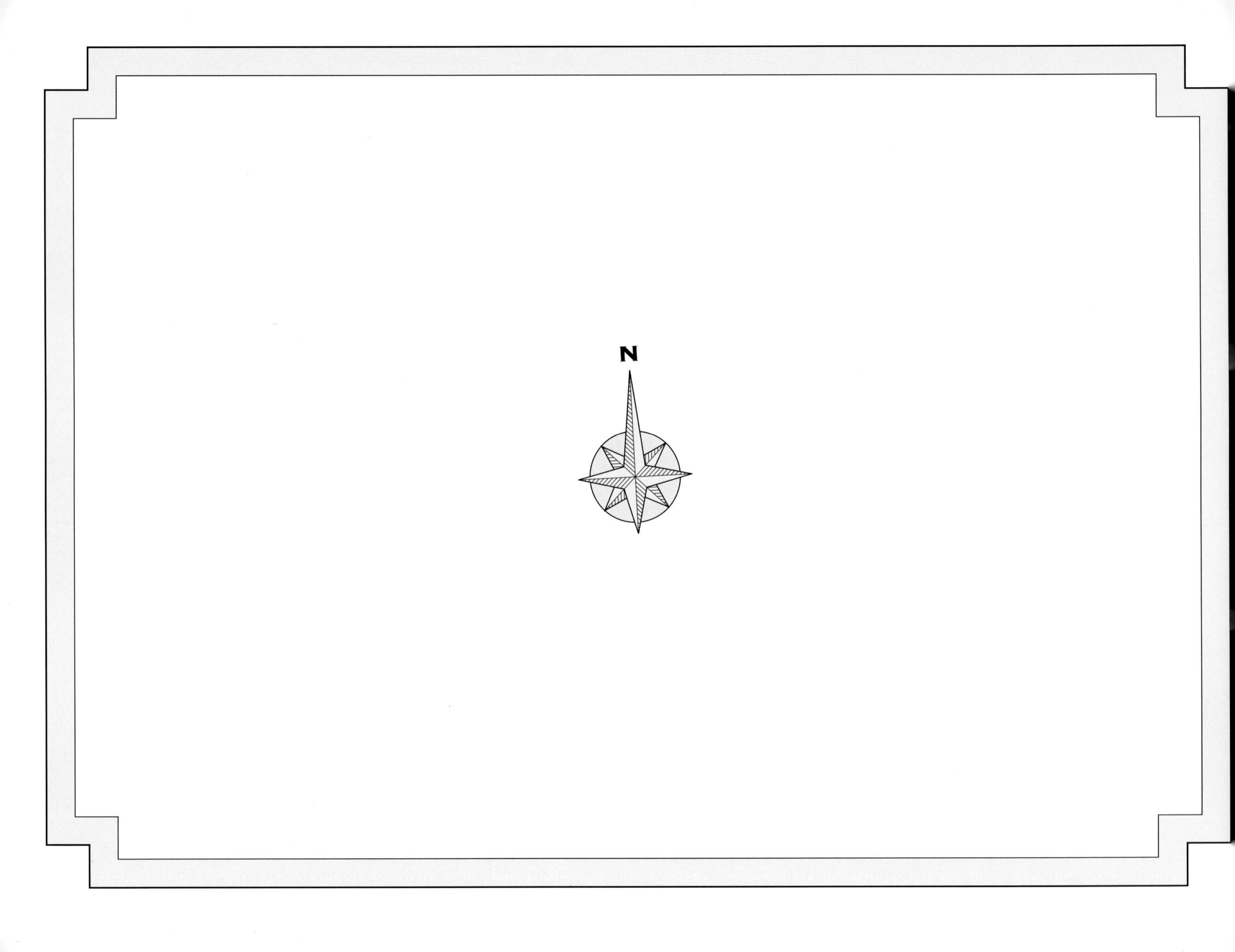
N

Boastful Maps

You Ain't Seen Nothin' Yet!

How vain, without the merit, is the name.
—HOMER

Town names:

1 - Seattle, WA
2 - Wenatchee, WA
3 - Colfax, WA
4 - Kelso, WA
5 - Hood River, OR
6 - Lincoln City, OR
7 - Albany, OR
8 - Newport, OR
9 - Eugene, OR
10 - Bandon, OR
11 - Smith River, CA
12 - Willits, CA
13 - Yuba City, CA
14 - Sacramento, CA
15 - Davis, CA
16 - Patterson, CA
17 - Bishop, CA
18 - Gilroy, CA
19 - Castroville, CA
20 - Greenfield, CA
21 - Lindsey, CA
22 - Parkfield, CA
23 - Pismo Beach, CA
24 - Lompoc, CA
25 - Indio, CA
26 - Fallbrook, CA
27 - Encinitas, CA
28 - Las Vegas, NV
29 - Blackfoot, ID
30 - Salmon, ID
31 - Lewiston, ID
32 - Wallace, ID
33 - Drummond, MT
34 - Glendive, MT
35 - Miles City, MT
36 - Crow Agency, MT
37 - Green River, WY
38 - Vernal, UT
39 - Moab, UT
40 - Wickenburg, AZ
41 - Hatch, NM
42 - Lovington, NM
43 - Grants, NM
44 - Albuquerque, NM
45 - Gallup, NM
46 - Dove Creek, CO
47 - Cozad, NE
48 - Central City, NE
49 - Omaha, NE
50 - Verdigre, NE
51 - Gayville, SD
52 - Pierre, SD
53 - Redfield, SD
54 - Mobridge, SD
55 - Hazleton, ND
56 - Devils Lake, ND
57 - Cando, ND
58 - Hibbing, MN
59 - Longville, MN
60 - Dorset, MN
61 - Anoka, MN
62 - Hopkins, MN
63 - Fulda, MN
64 - Dyersville, IA
65 - Knoxville, IA
66 - Olathe, KS
67 - La Crosse, KS
68 - Wichita, KS
69 - Dodge City, KS
70 - Wellington, KS
71 - Beaver, OK
72 - Jay, OK
73 - Kingston, OK
74 - Lubbock, TX
75 - Athens, TX
76 - San Saba, TX
77 - Austin, TX
78 - Rocksprings, TX
79 - Houston, TX
80 - Presidio, TX
81 - Crystal City, TX
82 - Aransas Pass, TX
83 - Bridge City, LA
84 - Gonzales, LA
85 - Rayne, LA
86 - Breaux Bridge, LA
87 - Greenwood, MS
88 - Malvern, AR
89 - Mount Ida, AR
90 - Stuttgart, AR
91 - Lonoke, AR
92 - Sarcoxie, MO
93 - Warsaw, MO
94 - Washington, MO
95 - Collinsville, IL
96 - Decatur, IL
97 - Morton, IL
98 - Kewanee, IL
99 - Rockford, IL
100 - Wautoma, WI
101 - Bloomer, WI
102 - Lake Tomahawk, WI
103 - Mercer, WI
104 - Mackinac Island, MI
105 - Traverse City, MI
106 - Battle Creek, MI
107 - Detroit, MI
108 - Colon, MI
109 - Peru, IN
110 - Van Buren, IN
111 - Bedford, IN
112 - Bardstown, KY
113 - Cadiz, KY
114 - Shelbyville, TN
115 - Memphis, TN
116 - Ft. Payne, AL
117 - Albertville, AL
118 - Dothan, AL
119 - Islamorada, FL
120 - Miami Beach, FL
121 - Lake Placid, FL
122 - Jensen Beach, FL
123 - Mulberry, FL
124 - Tarpon Springs, FL
125 - Apopka, FL
126 - Baxley, GA
127 - Claxton, GA
128 - Waynesboro, GA
129 - Gainesville, GA
130 - Dalton, GA
131 - Myrtle Beach, SC
132 - Franklin, NC
133 - Thomasville, NC
134 - High Point, NC
135 - Hatteras, NC
136 - Weldon, NC
137 - Martinsville, VA
138 - Suffolk, VA
139 - Wachapreague, VA
140 - Winchester, VA
141 - Richwood, WV
142 - Reynoldsburg, OH
143 - Hinckley, OH
144 - Wilkes-Barre, PA
145 - Punxsutawney, PA
146 - Ocean City, MD
147 - Wilmington, DE
148 - Vineland, NJ
149 - New York, NY
150 - Buffalo, NY
151 - Geneva, NY
152 - Niagara Falls, NY
153 - Hartford, CT
154 - Providence, RI
155 - Marblehead, MA
156 - Barre, VT
157 - St. Albans, VT
158 - Rumney, NH
159 - Rockland, ME
160 - Farmington, ME
161 - Cherryfield, ME
162 - Digby, *Canada*
163 - Blacks Harbour, *Canada*
164 - Tide Head, *Canada*
165 - Ste.-Anne-de-la-Pérade, *Canada*
166 - Ste.-Anne-des-Plaines, *Canada*
167 - Napanee, *Canada*
168 - Churchill, *Canada*
169 - Selkirk, *Canada*
170 - Campbell River, *Canada*
171 - Punta Abreojos, *Mexico*
172 - Tampico, *Mexico*

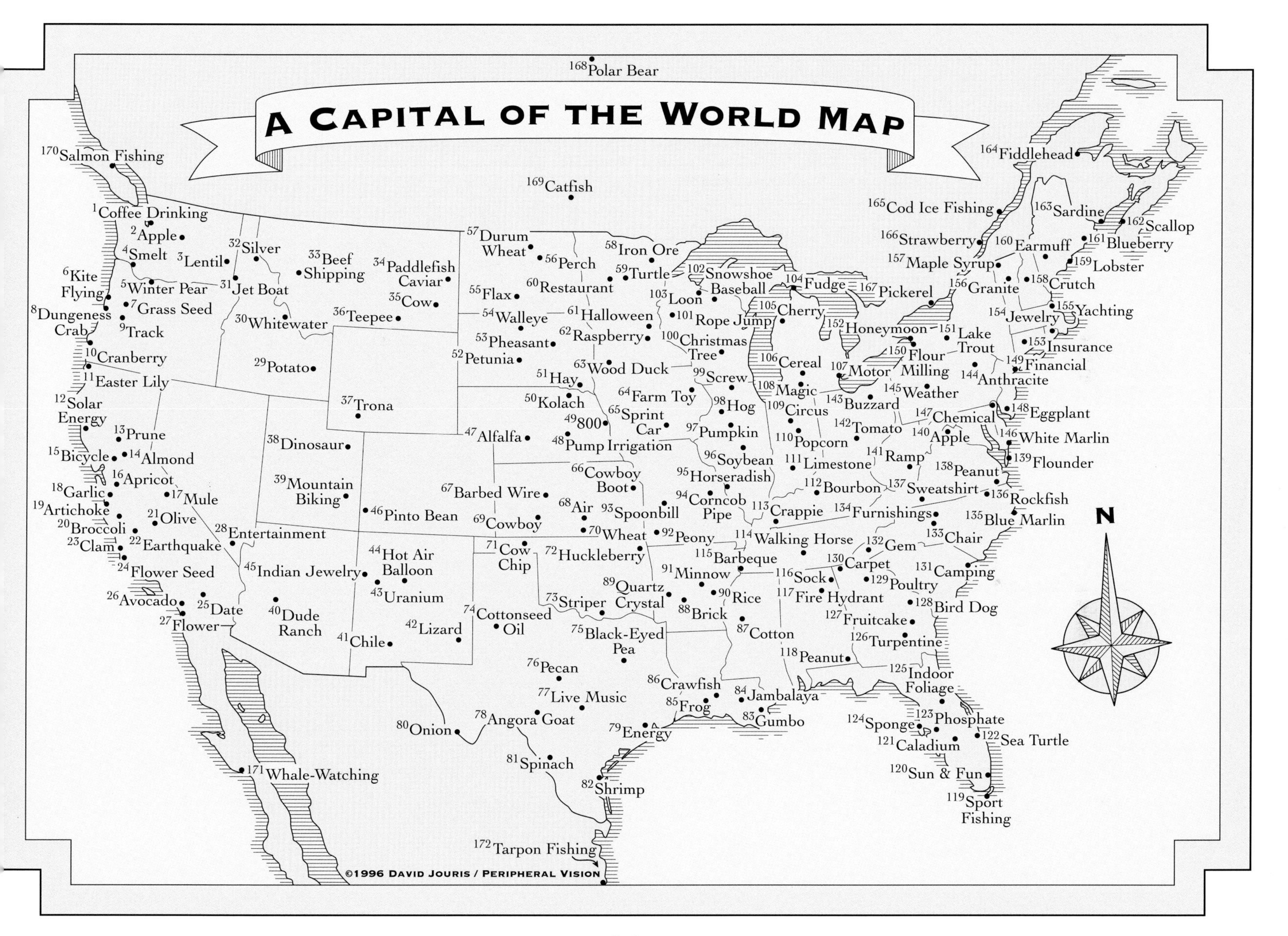
A Capital of the World Map
1 Coffee Drinking
2 Apple
3 Lentil
4 Smelt
5 Winter Pear
6 Kite Flying
7 Grass Seed
8 Dungeness Crab
9 Track
10 Cranberry
11 Easter Lily
12 Solar Energy
13 Prune
14 Almond
15 Bicycle
16 Apricot
17 Mule
18 Garlic
19 Artichoke
20 Broccoli
21 Olive
22 Earthquake
23 Clam
24 Flower Seed
25 Date
26 Avocado
27 Flower
28 Entertainment
29 Potato
30 Whitewater
31 Jet Boat
32 Silver
33 Beef Shipping
34 Paddlefish Caviar
35 Cow
36 Teepee
37 Trona
38 Dinosaur
39 Mountain Biking
40 Dude Ranch
41 Chile
42 Lizard
43 Uranium
44 Hot Air Balloon
45 Indian Jewelry
46 Pinto Bean
47 Alfalfa
48 Pump Irrigation
49 800
50 Kolach
51 Hay
52 Petunia
53 Pheasant
54 Walleye
55 Flax
56 Perch
57 Durum Wheat
58 Iron Ore
59 Turtle
60 Restaurant
61 Halloween
62 Raspberry
63 Wood Duck
64 Farm Toy
65 Sprint Car
66 Cowboy Boot
67 Barbed Wire
68 Air
69 Cowboy
70 Wheat
71 Cow Chip
72 Huckleberry
73 Striper
74 Cottonseed Oil
75 Black-Eyed Pea
76 Pecan
77 Live Music
78 Angora Goat
79 Energy
80 Onion
81 Spinach
82 Shrimp
83 Gumbo
84 Jambalaya
85 Frog
86 Crawfish
87 Cotton
88 Brick
89 Quartz Crystal
90 Rice
91 Minnow
92 Peony
93 Spoonbill
94 Corncob Pipe
95 Horseradish
96 Soybean
97 Pumpkin
98 Hog
99 Screw
100 Christmas Tree
101 Rope Jump
102 Snowshoe Baseball
103 Loon
104 Fudge
105 Cherry
106 Cereal
107 Motor
108 Magic
109 Circus
110 Popcorn
111 Limestone
112 Bourbon
113 Crappie
114 Walking Horse
115 Barbeque
116 Sock
117 Fire Hydrant
118 Peanut
119 Sport Fishing
120 Sun & Fun
121 Caladium
122 Sea Turtle
123 Phosphate
124 Sponge
125 Indoor Foliage
126 Turpentine
127 Fruitcake
128 Bird Dog
129 Poultry
130 Carpet
131 Camping
132 Gem
133 Chair
134 Furnishings
135 Blue Marlin
136 Rockfish
137 Sweatshirt
138 Peanut
139 Flounder
140 Apple
141 Ramp
142 Tomato
143 Buzzard
144 Anthracite
145 Weather
146 White Marlin
147 Chemical
148 Eggplant
149 Financial
150 Flour Milling
151 Lake Trout
152 Honeymoon
153 Insurance
154 Jewelry
155 Yachting
156 Granite
157 Maple Syrup
158 Crutch
159 Lobster
160 Earmuff
161 Blueberry
162 Scallop
163 Sardine
164 Fiddlehead
165 Cod Ice Fishing
166 Strawberry
167 Pickerel
168 Polar Bear
169 Catfish
170 Salmon Fishing
171 Whale-Watching
172 Tarpon Fishing
N
©1996 David Jouris / Peripheral Vision

You can tell the ideals of a nation by its advertisements.
—Norman Douglas

Never mistake the thing promoted for the thing itself.
—Howard Gossage

Formerly Derry Church, **Hershey, PA**, was renamed for native-son Milton Hershey in 1906 when he located his new chocolate factory there. Appropriately, the town's main thoroughfare is named Chocolate Avenue; some other streets in town are named for places where the cocoa bean comes from—Bahia, Caracas, and Granada.

Beatrice, NE, was originally home of the Beatrice Creamery Company. Founded in the 1890s, the company has grown into Beatrice Foods, one of the largest food companies in the world. Beatrice now makes such products as Dannon® yogurt, Mother's® cookies, Tropicana® fruit drinks, and Milk Duds.® The company has also diversified to include some other well-known, but less edible, products including Samsonite® luggage and Airstream® trailers.

In the early 1870s John Michael Kohler purchased his father-in-law's iron foundry (principally producing agricultural equipment) in Shebnoygan, WI. When the process for enamel-coated cast iron was developed a few years later, Kohler turned to making plumbing fixtures. Shortly before his death in 1900, Kohler bought land a few miles away and relocated his operations there. In the subsequent decades, the business continued under Kohler's son, Walter, who spearheaded the creation of a well-planned company town, **Kohler, WI**, next to the manufacturing site.

Philip Armour left his home, a farm near Stockbridge, NY, at 20 and walked to California to take part in the Gold Rush. But instead of mining for gold, he set up a butcher shop in Placerville, CA. When the boom in California started to fade, Armour moved to Milwaukee and built his meat packing empire. **Armour, SD**, was named for Philip Armour when the town was founded in 1886. Acknowledging this honor, Armour gave a bell for the town church. One of his friends in Placerville, incidently, was a man who profited from the gold rush by making wheelbarrows for the miners—John Studebaker, who later took his profits to Indiana and began a transportation company that built wagons and eventually cars.

Finally, it's worth mentioning here that Fig Newtons® were first produced by the Kennedy Biscuit Works of Massachusetts, in 1892. The company had a practice of taking the names for its products from the towns around Boston; Newton, MA, just happened to be next in line. The "Fig" was added later, when figs became the most common filling.

A BRAND NAME MAP
Danskin
Comet
Lipton
Acme
Carnation
Du Pont
Yale
Tide
Wonder
Haines
Durkee
Avon
Pinnacle
Alhambra
Heath
Peerless
Cascade
Dell
Leslie
Arco
Parker
Burlington
Hathaway
Gillette
Stanley
Colgate
Halma
Pillsbury
Weber
Land O'Lakes
Wausau
Oshkosh
Beacon
Sears
Kohler
Kellogg
Hoover
Polo
Armour
Superior
Midas
Lee
Wilson
Challenge
Hilton
Pioneer
Delta
Aurora
Sterling
Firestone
Aspen
Champion
Springfield
Beatrice
Glade
Goodrich
Zenith
Partridge
West Bend
Glidden
Corning
Revere
Regal
Case
Dove
Fisk
Timberline
Remington
Aetna
Bud
Excello
Campbell
Mars
Atlas
Butler
Next
Brand
Wilkinson
Lego
Ajax
Crown
Arista
Kodak
Raleigh
Bunn
Dewars
Norton
Stratford
Stetson
Frye
Rockport
Côte d'Or
Borden
Oneida
Ocean Spray
Kenmore
Eagle
Hunter
Bantam
Clark
Commodore
Hershey
Dover
Cannon
Norge
Atlantic
Delco
Shell
Pendleton
Brand
Gibson
Westwood
Sunsweet
Armstrong
Coleman
Hollywood
Glory
Alcoa
Waring
Underwood
Hamilton
Arrowhead
Wesson
Lux
Baldwin
Fender
Bissell
Tandy
Joy
Orion
Bosco
Ball
Singer
Bon Ami
Ace
Sealy
Anchor
Converse
Coke
Domino
Kenwood
Sperry
Dow
Spaulding
Apple
Sunkist
Dial
Morton
Vera
Post
Admiral
Canon
Progresso
Otis
Rodeo
Blue Diamond
Bell
El Toro
Crest
Goodyear
Globe
Crane
Alamo
El Toro
Corona
N
©1996 DAVID JOURIS / PERIPHERAL VISION

America is rather like life. You can usually find in it what you look for.... It will probably be interesting, and it is sure to be large.

—E. M. FORESTER

The name for the small community of **Titanic, OK**, was taken to honor the famous ocean liner that sank after hitting an iceberg in April of 1912. Over 1,500 people were drowned in the icy water off Newfoundland in this colossal disaster. The word "titanic" originated from a mythological family of giants—the Titans—featured in early Greek legends. (By the way, the tallest *non-mythological* person on record was born in Alton, IL, in 1918; Robert Wadlow was just under 9 feet tall when he died in 1940.)

Located near the south rim of the huge geological formation for which it is named is **Grand Canyon, AZ**. Spanish explorers used the word *cañon* (literally "pipe") for the enormous fissures in the earth that they found in the American Southwest. And as they came upon the greatest one, they could only describe it as the *grande cañon*, or "great pipe." English-speaking Americans have slightly anglicised the name.

The tiny village of **Jumbo, AR**, was meant to be named for a local resident, Jimbo Smith, but the name was somehow garbled by the Post Office Department. The confusion may be partly attributed to the timing; this happened not long after the word "jumbo" entered the English language as a result of the fame of a certain African elephant. (In the early 1880s, P. T. Barnum exhibited Jumbo to millions of Americans.) As the largest animal in captivity at the time—over 11½ feet tall and weighing 6½ tons—Jumbo's name became synonymous with "mammoth," itself a term for a kind of elephant.

Mammoth, AZ, was named for the Mammoth Mine located there, itself named after "a mammoth copper ledge." **Mammoth, UT**, took its name from yet another Mammoth Mine, so called because of a large outcropping indicating its veins of rich ore. Utah's Mammoth Mine, located in the mountains near the town, produced gold, silver, copper, and lead.

And speaking of elephants, let's not forget that **Big Bone, KY**, got its name when large fossil bones of mastodons were discovered there.

A Great Big Map
Titanic
Massive
Big Farm
Grand Isle
Big Lots
Great Pond
Big Beaver
Grand Coulee
Bigfork
Big Sandy
Grandview
Grand Forks
Big Falls
Grand Marais
Grand Mound
La Grande
Big Arm
Grandview
Orogrande
Bighorn
Big Timber
Big Sky
Big Bend
Great Bend
Big Lake
Grand View
Big Bay
Big Moose
Great Boars Head
Grand Beach
Grand Ronde
Big Creek
Gross
Big Stone City
Big Rock
Grand Gorge
Great Barrington
Grand View
Big Little Acres
Big Horn
Big Bend
Grand Meadow
Grand Marsh
Grand Rapids
Big Tree
Big Indian
Great Valley
Great Neck
Big Sandy
Big Springs
Big Patch
Grosse Pointe
Biggerville
Great Meadows
Big Bar
Big Piney
Gross
Grand Junction
Big Foot
Grand Detour
Big Prairie
Giant Oaks
Rio Grande
Big Springs
Grand Island
Grand River
Big Rock
Big Plain
Big Pool
Big Mills Bridge
Big Chief
Mammoth
Big Elk Meadows
Tall Timbers
Big Neck
Mammoth
Great Mills
Big Meadows
Grand Center
Big Bone
Major
Big Basin
Mammoth Lakes
Grand Vu
Grand Junction
Big Bend
Great Bend
Big Springs
Grand Pass
Grand Tower
Grandview
Big Four
Big Fork
Big Water
Grand Summit
Big River Mills
Big Ready
Grandfather
Grandview
Big Bow
Big Mountain
Big Cove
Big Lick
Arroyo Grande
Big Cabin
Jumbo
Grand Canyon
Big Flat
Big Boy Junction
Great Falls
Big Bear
Rio Grande Estates
Titanic
Grand Glaise
Big Canoe
Big Square
Grandfield
Big Cedar
Big Oak
Grand Terrace
Superior
Gran Quivira
Big Fork
Big Creek
Big Springs
Casa Grande
Big Springs
Mammoth
Grand Prairie
Grand Saline
Grand Cane
Grand Gulf
Big Creek
Greaterville
Orogrande
Big Spring
Grand Ridge
Gross
Big Level
Grandview
Grosse Tete
Bigpoint
Casa Grande
Grandfalls
Big Lake
El Cuervo Grande
Grand Chenier
Grand Caillou
Grand Island
Bigfoot
Big Wells
Gran Morelos
Rio Grande City
Ciénega Grande
©1996 David Jouris / Peripheral Vision
N

A fever of newness has been everywhere
confused with the spirit of progress.
—HENRY FORD

New Town, ND, was first named Newtown because it was a new town site that the government set up when a big dam was built nearby. Several towns were located in the area to be flooded, so the townsfolk were relocated to a dry location, but they just did not like the name Newtown. They were satisfied, however, when the name was slightly altered to New Town. Still, the newer name seems fairly dull, considering that the proximity of a dam could have lead to any number of interesting possibilities—as evidenced by the good citizens of Stockton, MO, who proclaim their home "the best town in the state by a dam site!"

In the 1870s, **New Era, MI**, was a logging community. When residents were establishing a town, the owner of the sawmill, who had come from Erie, PA, suggested naming the town New Erie. This was greeted by a noticeable lack of enthusiasm on the part of the locals, who preferred not to honor any particular person or place. New Era was settled on as a pleasing compromise, as it sounded similar to New Erie, yet acknowledged the beginning of a proper town with its own post office—in essence, the beginning of a new era.

As it turns out, **Newport News, VA**, is a corruption of the original name. The most persuasive story is that the town was originally named by Daniel Gookin, one of the early arrivals in Virginia from Ireland, who began a plantation there. A compatriot of Gookin's, Captain William Newce, had previously obtained a land grant nearby and had been made marshal of the colony. Newce's brother, Thomas, also had a plantation in the area and served as a local deputy. The Newces worked closely with Gookin to help run the new colony and to defend it against attack. Gookin apparently named the new port town he founded New Port Newce to honor the brothers. Over time, the first two words of the name melded into one (aided by the fact that Captain Christopher Newport had conveyed the settlers who founded the first English settlement at Jamestown, Virginia), and the last part was altered into a similar-sounding but more familiar word.

Newville, AL, was originally named Wells. Unfortunately for the town, there was already another community named Wells in the state, which made Wells unacceptable to postal authorities. Apparently the residents found it difficult to think of a more imaginative name, so they adopted Newville.

The common belief is that the name of **Newborn, GA**, came as a result of a successful religious revival in the town in the 1800s. It is said the large number of converts inspired the citizens to adopt the name. A minor problem with this compelling story: the town was named Newborn *before* the revival took place.

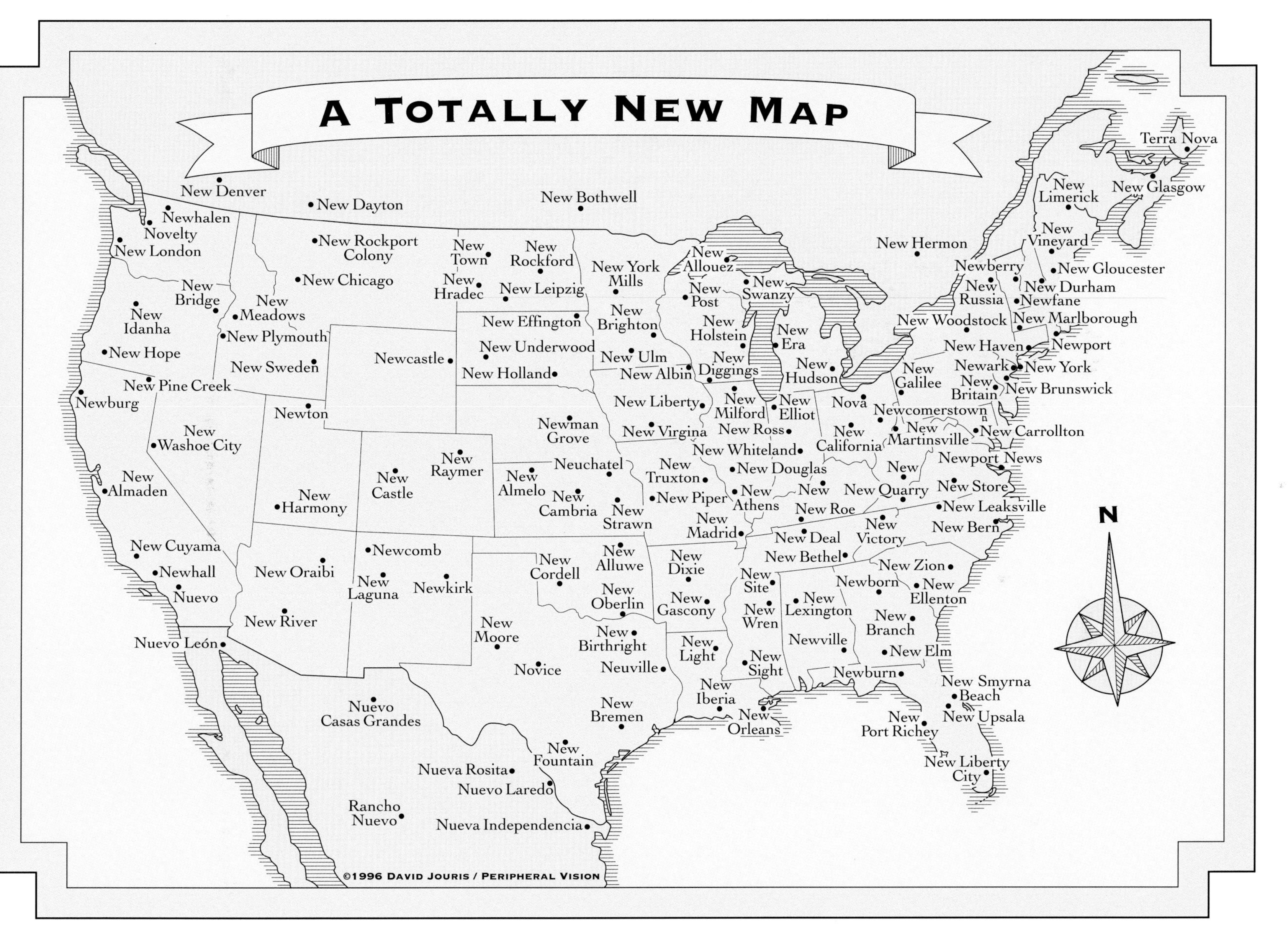
A Totally New Map
New Denver
New Dayton
New Bothwell
Terra Nova
New Glasgow
New Limerick
Newhalen
Novelty
New London
New Rockport Colony
New Town
New Rockford
New York Mills
New Allouez
New Hermon
New Vineyard
New Gloucester
Newberry
New Durham
New Russia
Newfane
New Bridge
New Chicago
New Hradec
New Leipzig
New Post
New Swanzy
New Idanha
New Meadows
New Plymouth
New Effington
New Brighton
New Holstein
New Era
New Woodstock
New Marlborough
New Hope
New Sweden
Newcastle
New Underwood
New Ulm
New Diggings
New Haven
Newport
New Holland
New Albin
New Hudson
New Galilee
Newark
New York
New Pine Creek
New Britain
New Brunswick
Newburg
Newton
New Liberty
New Milford
New Elliot
Nova
Newcomerstown
New Washoe City
Newman Grove
New Virgina
New Ross
New California
New Martinsville
New Carrollton
New Raymer
New Whiteland
Newport News
New Almaden
New Castle
New Almelo
Neuchatel
New Truxton
New Douglas
New
New Store
New Harmony
New Cambria
New Strawn
New Piper
New Athens
New
New Quarry
New Leaksville
New Roe
New Madrid
New Victory
New Bern
New Deal
New Cuyama
Newcomb
New Cordell
New Alluwe
New Dixie
New Bethel
New Zion
Newhall
New Oraibi
New Laguna
Newkirk
New Site
Newborn
New Ellenton
Nuevo
New Oberlin
New Gascony
New Lexington
New Wren
New Branch
New River
New Moore
Nuevo León
New Birthright
New Light
Newville
New Elm
New Sight
Novice
Neuville
Newburn
New Smyrna Beach
New Iberia
Nuevo Casas Grandes
New Bremen
New Orleans
New Upsala
New Port Richey
New Fountain
New Liberty City
Nueva Rosita
Nuevo Laredo
Rancho Nuevo
Nueva Independencia
N
©1996 David Jouris / Peripheral Vision

A map of the world that does not include Utopia
is not worth glancing at.
—Oscar Wilde

Utopia is what the imagination of man has to say
about the possibilities of the human spirit.
—Howard Thurman

Between the War of Independence and World War I, more than 250 utopian communites were started in the United States. A large number of the religion-based communities set up in the eighteenth and nineteenth centuries were predicated on a theory that a thousand-year-long Golden Age would arrive once a utopian society was set up. Sadly for these idealists, something always seemed to tear those "perfect" communities apart. (This brings to mind Randall Jarrell's statement that no matter how golden an age is, there will always be someone who complains that everything looks too yellow.)

Two religious groups begun in the mid 1800s managed to thrive due to their manufacturing. The communal society of **Oneida, NY**, was better known in the beginning, however, for its efforts to move away from monogamous marriage on the theory that, in a perfect society, people should love each other equally. After 25 years, the community changed its structure, eventually becoming the well-known silverware company it is today. The group at **Amana, IA**, managed to last until the Depression before they changed their ownership structure and became a maker of refrigerators and such.

It is said that at the time the name **Paradise, CA**, was chosen, there was an establishment in town called the Pair O' Dice Saloon—a place that no doubt tried to provide its own version of heaven on earth. And on at least one early map, the town name is actually spelled "Paradice." (Just down the road, too, once stood a place named Helltown.) Casting some doubt on the accuracy of these facts is a similar story told about the naming of **Paradise, MT**.

Avalon, PA, was named during a period when a Tennyson poem—*Idylls of the King*—made the word (albeit with a slightly different spelling) well known. Etymologically, the name Avalon is related to the Celtic word for "apple," and the town is situated, appropriately enough, in a former apple orchard. **Avalon, CA**, is located on an island off the coast, similar to the legendary final resting place of King Arthur.

Utopia, TX, is said to have gotten its name because of its "ideal location and climate." The origin of the name of the tiny community of **Utopia, PA**, has since faded into obscurity, and the community itself has practically disappeared.

Arcosanti, AZ, is a community created by Paolo Soleri and a group of volunteers in 1970. Based on Soleri's visionary ideas, this urban habitat aims to integrate ecological concepts with city life—thus it features a large greenhouse but has no cars.

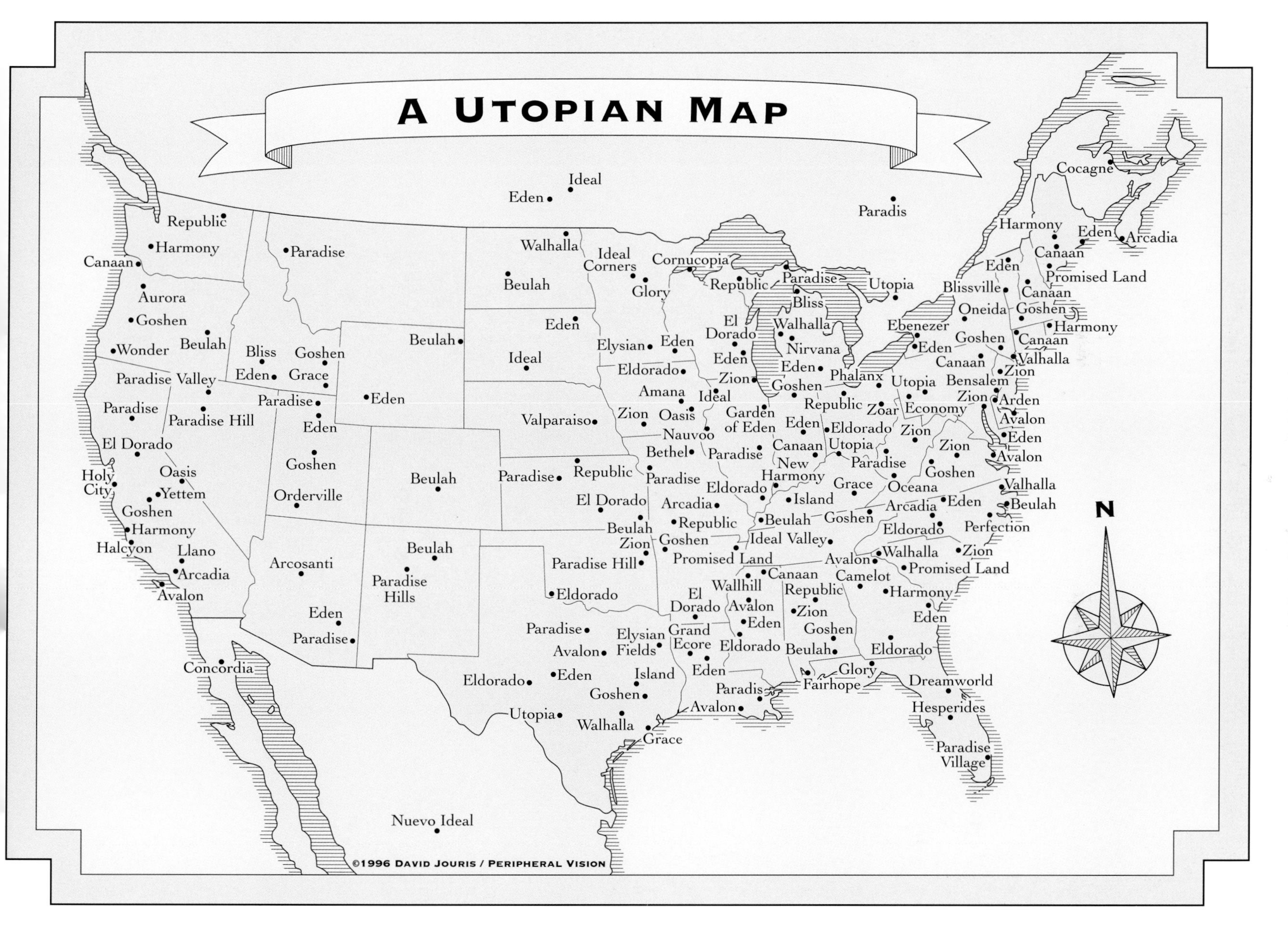
A Utopian Map
Ideal
Eden
Paradis
Cocagne
Harmony
Eden
Arcadia
Canaan
Eden
Promised Land
Republic
Harmony
Paradise
Canaan
Walhalla
Ideal Corners
Cornucopia
Beulah
Glory
Republic
Paradise
Utopia
Blissville
Canaan
Bliss
Aurora
Goshen
Oneida
Goshen
Harmony
El Dorado
Walhalla
Ebenezer
Eden
Beulah
Beulah
Elysian
Eden
Nirvana
Goshen
Canaan
Wonder
Bliss
Goshen
Eden
Eden
Canaan
Valhalla
Ideal
Eldorado
Eden
Zion
Phalanx
Utopia
Bensalem
Grace
Paradise Valley
Eden
Zion
Goshen
Amana
Ideal
Republic
Zion
Arden
Paradise
Eden
Paradise
Zoar
Economy
Paradise Hill
Eden
Valparaiso
Zion
Oasis
Garden of Eden
Eden
Eldorado
Zion
Avalon
Nauvoo
Eden
El Dorado
Bethel
Paradise
Canaan
Utopia
Zion
Avalon
Goshen
New Harmony
Paradise
Goshen
Holy City
Oasis
Beulah
Paradise
Republic
Paradise
Eldorado
Grace
Oceana
Valhalla
Yettem
Orderville
El Dorado
Arcadia
Island
Arcadia
Eden
Beulah
Goshen
Republic
Beulah
Goshen
Harmony
Beulah
Eldorado
Perfection
Halcyon
Llano
Goshen
Ideal Valley
Beulah
Zion
Walhalla
Zion
Arcosanti
Paradise Hill
Promised Land
Avalon
Promised Land
Arcadia
Paradise Hills
Canaan
Camelot
Avalon
Wallhill
Republic
Harmony
Eldorado
El Dorado
Avalon
Zion
Eden
Eden
Paradise
Eden
Grand Ecore
Goshen
Elysian Fields
Paradise
Eldorado
Beulah
Eldorado
Avalon
Concordia
Eden
Glory
Eldorado
Eden
Island
Fairhope
Dreamworld
Goshen
Paradis
Avalon
Hesperides
Utopia
Walhalla
Grace
Paradise Village
Nuevo Ideal
N
©1996 David Jouris / Peripheral Vision

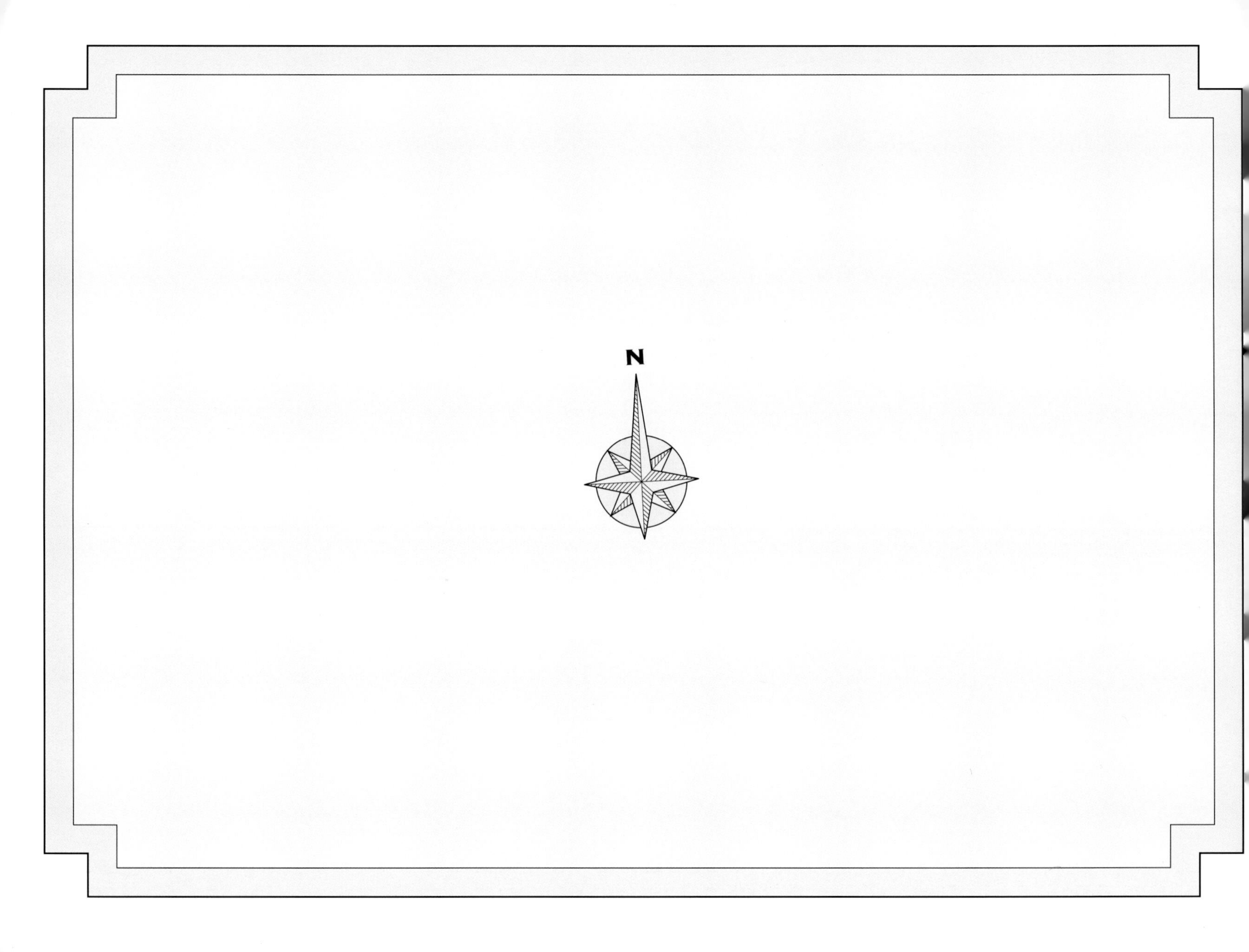
N

Artistic Maps

What in the Name of Creation Is Going on Here?

The sense of being well-dressed gives a feeling of inward tranquility which religion is powerless to bestow.
—C. F. FORBES

You win some, you lose some, but you gotta get dressed for 'em all.
—SUSAN KENNEY

Tuxedo Park, NY, began as a resort near Tuxedo Lake, forty miles northwest of New York City. There, at an autumn ball in 1886, a young fellow named Griswold Lorillard wore a tailless dress coat that has since become known as a tuxedo. The dinner jacket, sporting satin lapels and tailored along the lines of fox-hunting jackets, was designed by his father. It was not exactly an instant success; it is said that at least one critic suggested Lorillard was better suited for a straitjacket.

Although "capa" means a circular cloak or bullfighter's cape, **Capa, SD**, probably took its name from the Sioux Indian word for "beaver," due to the large number of those animals living along the nearby river, though some residents seem to prefer a more creative explanation for the town name, thereby making something out of whole cloth. They report that in the early part of this century, when the regional railroad began routing freight through the area, the train cars had the word "capacity" painted on the doors, divided so that "capa" appeared on one door and "city" on the other. The town was called Capa City for a while, before it was shortened to just Capa.

Wooden Shoe Village, MI, got its name during a time when loggers from Ohio came there to work. To ward off their powerful thirst, these bronzed American working men brought along their favorite brand of beer—and all too often left the empties laying around. The litterbugs' beer of preference was called Wooden Shoe.

Bloomer, WI, was named for a wealthy merchant who bought land there to set up a mill in the mid 1800s. This same era also saw a big change in the world of women's fashion. The modified Turkish-style trousers named after Amelia Jenks Bloomer (no relation to the merchant), were actually first made by Gerrit Smith, whose daughter Elizabeth Smith Miller was the first to wear them. Amelia Bloomer was editor of *The Lily*, the first women's magazine in America; she was a pioneer of the women's rights movement and championed the cause of dress reform. At the time, fashion decreed voluminous hoopskirts for women; Bloomer helped to change this by including patterns for Gerrit Smith's design in *The Lily*—thus permanently linking her own name to the new fashion.

Amasa Stetson of Massachusetts bought the land that is now **Stetson, ME**, a town named after him. It was John Batterson Stetson of Philadelphia, however, who made the hat that carries this famous name. (This is probably the place to mention that a ten-gallon hat does not refer to the cubic capacity of such a hat, but rather to the number of braided ribbons (Spanish *galón*) that decorate it. The bigger the hat, the more room for ribbons.)

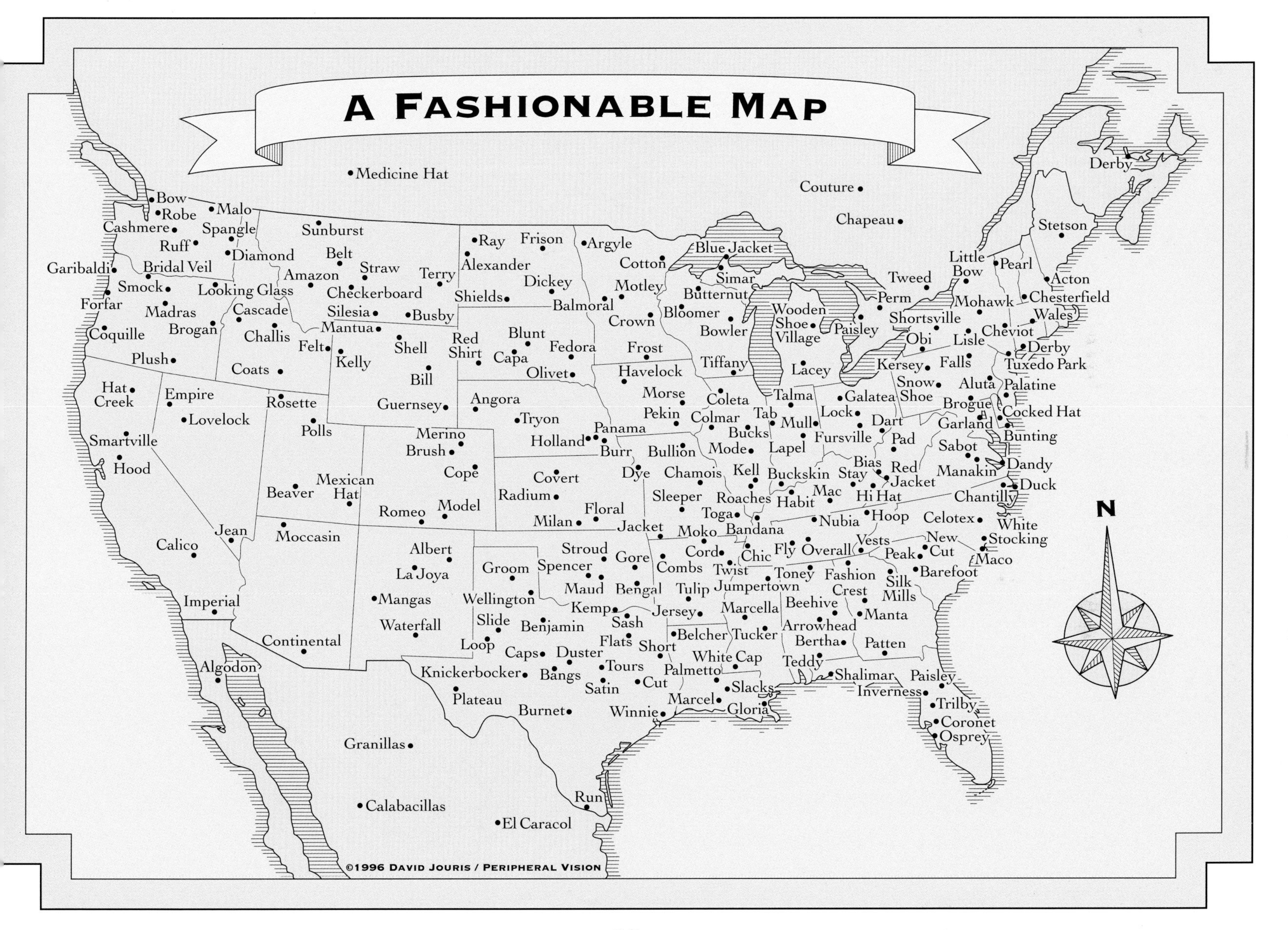
A FASHIONABLE MAP
Medicine Hat
Couture
Derby
Chapeau
Stetson
Bow
Robe
Malo
Cashmere
Spangle
Sunburst
Ruff
Diamond
Ray
Frison
Argyle
Blue Jacket
Garibaldi
Bridal Veil
Belt
Alexander
Cotton
Simar
Little Bow
Pearl
Tweed
Acton
Smock
Amazon
Straw
Terry
Dickey
Motley
Butternut
Perm
Mohawk
Chesterfield
Forfar
Looking Glass
Checkerboard
Shields
Balmoral
Bloomer
Wooden Shoe Village
Shortsville
Wales
Madras
Cascade
Silesia
Busby
Crown
Bowler
Paisley
Obi
Lisle
Cheviot
Coquille
Brogan
Challis
Mantua
Red Shirt
Blunt
Derby
Felt
Shell
Capa
Fedora
Frost
Kersey
Falls
Tuxedo Park
Kelly
Tiffany
Lacey
Plush
Coats
Havelock
Olivet
Bill
Snow
Aluta
Palatine
Hat Creek
Empire
Rosette
Guernsey
Angora
Morse
Coleta
Talma
Galatea
Shoe
Brogue
Cocked Hat
Lovelock
Polls
Tryon
Pekin
Colmar
Tab
Mull
Lock
Dart
Garland
Merino
Panama
Bucks
Fursville
Bunting
Smartville
Brush
Holland
Burr
Bullion
Mode
Lapel
Pad
Sabot
Hood
Cope
Dye
Chamois
Kell
Buckskin
Bias
Stay
Red Jacket
Manakin
Dandy
Mexican Hat
Covert
Mac
Duck
Beaver
Radium
Sleeper
Roaches
Habit
Hi Hat
Chantilly
Model
Floral
Toga
Romeo
Milan
Nubia
Hoop
Celotex
White Stocking
Jean
Moccasin
Jacket
Moko
Bandana
Calico
Albert
Stroud
Vests
New Cut
Gore
Cord
Chic
Fly
Overall
Peak
Maco
Groom
Spencer
La Joya
Combs
Twist
Toney
Fashion
Barefoot
Maud
Bengal
Tulip
Jumpertown
Silk Mills
Crest
Imperial
Mangas
Wellington
Kemp
Jersey
Marcella
Beehive
Manta
Sash
Waterfall
Slide
Benjamin
Arrowhead
Continental
Belcher
Tucker
Bertha
Patten
Flats
Loop
Short
Caps
Duster
White Cap
Teddy
Algodon
Tours
Palmetto
Shalimar
Paisley
Knickerbocker
Bangs
Cut
Inverness
Satin
Slacks
Plateau
Marcel
Trilby
Burnet
Winnie
Gloria
Coronet
Osprey
Granillas
Run
Calabacillas
El Caracol
N
©1996 DAVID JOURIS / PERIPHERAL VISION

The structure of a play is always the story of how the birds came home to roost.
—ARTHUR MILLER

The theater is the most beautiful place on earth.
—ANNE BANCROFT

Judge Roy Bean was appointed Justice of the Peace in Vinegaroon in 1882 to maintain law and order in construction camps along the Southern Pacific Railroad. For years Bean was known as "the only law west of the Pecos" (although it should be pointed out that he presided in a town only a few miles west of said river). The judge was an ardent admirer of the British stage actress Lily Langtry; it is often said that when he became Justice of the Peace he renamed the town **Langtry, TX**. Another source says that Bean did not arrive in town until 1885, four years after the town had already been named Langtry, in honor of a young English civil engineer on a survey crew for the railroad. You be the judge.

The name of **Chautauqua, NY**, comes from efforts to spell a Seneca Indian word whose meaning is uncertain. (The many possibilities include "two moccasins tied together," "place where one is lost," "foggy place," and "fish taken out.") The town began as the site of an adult-education program founded in the 1800s, and the very word "chautauqua" came to mean an institution that aspired to improve body, mind, and spirit with a program that included lectures, discussions, entertainment, and readings. In the early part of the twentieth century, traveling chautauquas—whose brown canvas tents made them easily distinguishable from the white tents used by circuses and other circuit theater groups—toured across the country, visiting communities whose citizens had little in the way of diversion and had a hunger for more richness in their lives.

Long Run, PA, turns out not to be named for some notably long engagment by a theater company. The term "run" is used here to mean "creek." Apparently, in this region with myriad streams and creeks, there is one that stretches for quite an impressive distance.

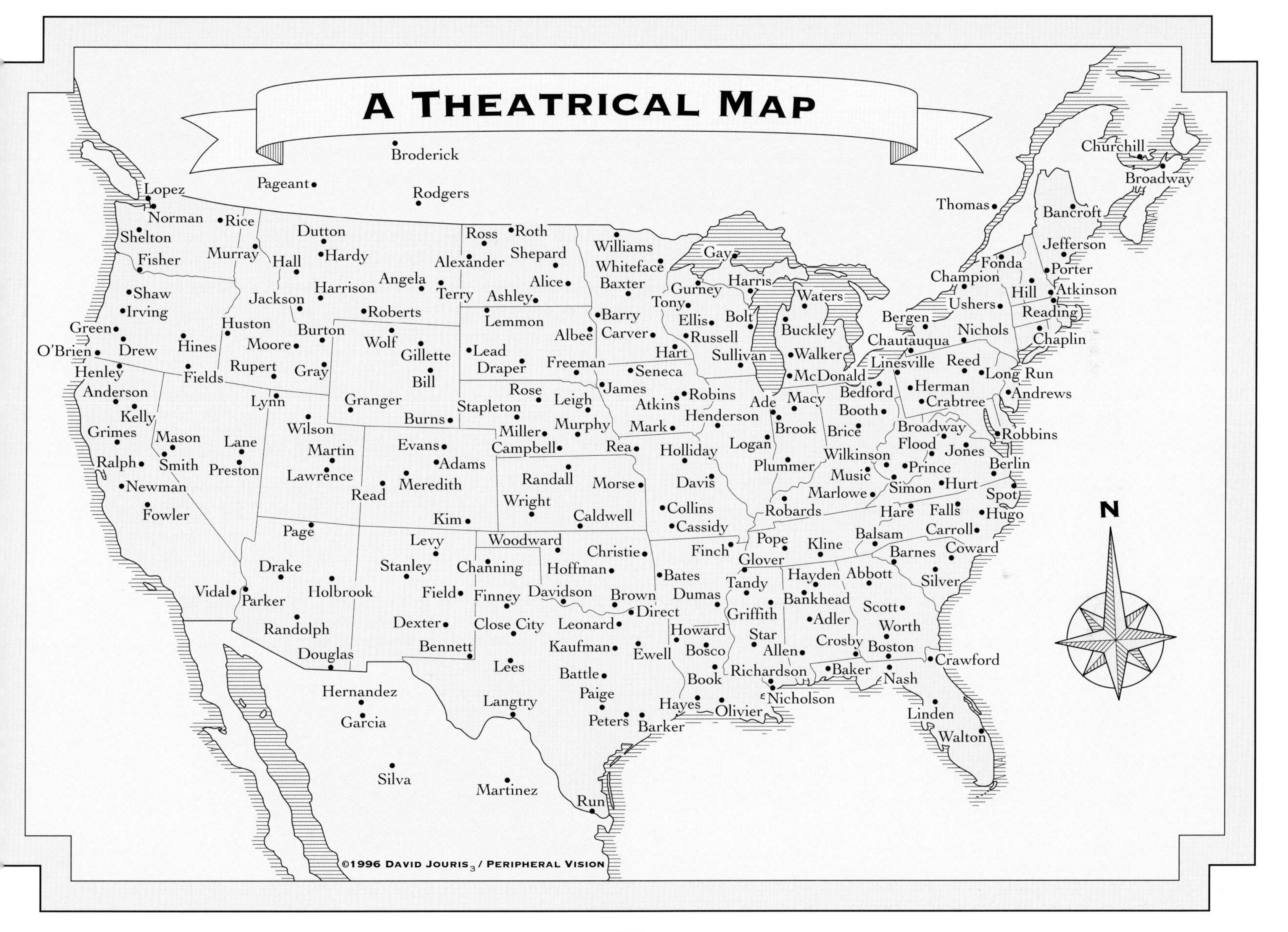
A THEATRICAL MAP
Broderick
Pageant
Rodgers
Lopez
Norman
Rice
Shelton
Fisher
Murray
Hall
Dutton
Hardy
Ross
Roth
Alexander
Shepard
Williams
Whiteface
Gay
Harris
Churchill
Broadway
Thomas
Bancroft
Jefferson
Porter
Fonda
Champion
Hill
Atkinson
Shaw
Irving
Harrison
Angela
Terry
Alice
Ashley
Baxter
Gurney
Tony
Waters
Ushers
Reading
Jackson
Roberts
Lemmon
Barry
Ellis
Bolt
Bergen
Nichols
Chaplin
Green
Huston
Burton
Wolf
Albee
Carver
Russell
Buckley
Chautauqua
O'Brien
Drew
Hines
Moore
Gillette
Lead
Hart
Sullivan
Walker
Linesville
Reed
Long Run
Henley
Fields
Rupert
Gray
Draper
Freeman
Seneca
McDonald
Bill
James
Herman
Andrews
Anderson
Lynn
Granger
Rose
Leigh
Atkins
Robins
Ade
Macy
Bedford
Crabtree
Kelly
Burns
Stapleton
Henderson
Booth
Grimes
Mason
Wilson
Miller
Murphy
Mark
Brook
Brice
Broadway
Robbins
Lane
Martin
Evans
Campbell
Rea
Holliday
Logan
Flood
Jones
Ralph
Smith
Preston
Adams
Wilkinson
Prince
Berlin
Lawrence
Plummer
Music
Newman
Read
Meredith
Randall
Morse
Davis
Marlowe
Simon
Hurt
Spot
Fowler
Wright
Collins
Robards
Hare
Falls
Hugo
Kim
Caldwell
Cassidy
Balsam
Carroll
Page
Levy
Woodward
Christie
Finch
Pope
Kline
Barnes
Coward
Drake
Stanley
Channing
Hoffman
Glover
Bates
Hayden
Abbott
Silver
Vidal
Parker
Holbrook
Field
Finney
Davidson
Brown
Dumas
Tandy
Bankhead
Scott
Direct
Griffith
Adler
Randolph
Dexter
Close City
Leonard
Howard
Worth
Star
Crosby
Bennett
Kaufman
Ewell
Bosco
Allen
Boston
Crawford
Douglas
Lees
Battle
Richardson
Baker
Nash
Book
Hernandez
Paige
Nicholson
Langtry
Hayes
Olivier
Linden
Garcia
Peters
Barker
Walton
Silva
Martinez
Run
N
©1996 DAVID JOURIS3 / PERIPHERAL VISION

All men's misfortune, and the appalling disasters of history,
the blunders of statesmen and the errors of great generals,
come from the inability to dance.
—**JEAN MOLIÈRE**

I delight in all manifestations of the terpsichorean muse.
—**JOHN CLEESE**

Charles II, the British king during the later part of the 1600s, gave his name to the town of **Charleston, SC**, and the town went on to give its name to the lively ballroom dance of the 1920s. Several other dances also originated in South Carolina and went on to sweep the country, including "the big apple"—a large circle dance—originated at an African-American nightclub in Columbia, SC. And let's not overlook the intriguingly named "peeling the peach"—a now almost-forgotten dance that began at the summer resort of Myrtle Beach, SC.

The name of **Quantico, VA**, comes from an Indian word meaning "dancing" or "place of dancing." Quantico is now the site of the U. S. Marine Corps training facility. One would hear *taps* at Quantico at the end of the day, but it really isn't a place of dancing now.

When the waltz was introduced in the late 1700s, it ushered in a bold new concept: partners danced while facing each other in "a close embrace position." As curious as it may seem now, the dance was assailed at the time for such "moral laxity." **Waltz, MI**, however, was named for Josiah Waltz, who laid out the town in 1872; **Waltz, PA**, was named for Jacob Waltz, who established a mill and distillery in the 1790s, and also served as the first postmaster.

Mexican Hat, UT, has no relation to the famous Mexican dance. The name comes from a large geological formation near the town. Rising some 200 feet above the valley floor, this formation is capped by much wider rock, which resembles a Mexican sombrero.

Settlers in southeastern Michigan set up a school in the mid 1800s called the Disco Academy. This wasn't a place that taught the latest dances, but rather took its name from the Latin verb meaning "I learn." The village of **Disco, MI**, is named after this school.

Sundance, WY, takes its name from nearby Sundance Mountain where, according to Sioux legend, the first sun dance was held. It is from this town (located in Crook County, by the way) that the outlaw called the Sundance Kid took his nickname. One writer has suggested that "from all appearances that was the only thing in town worth taking."

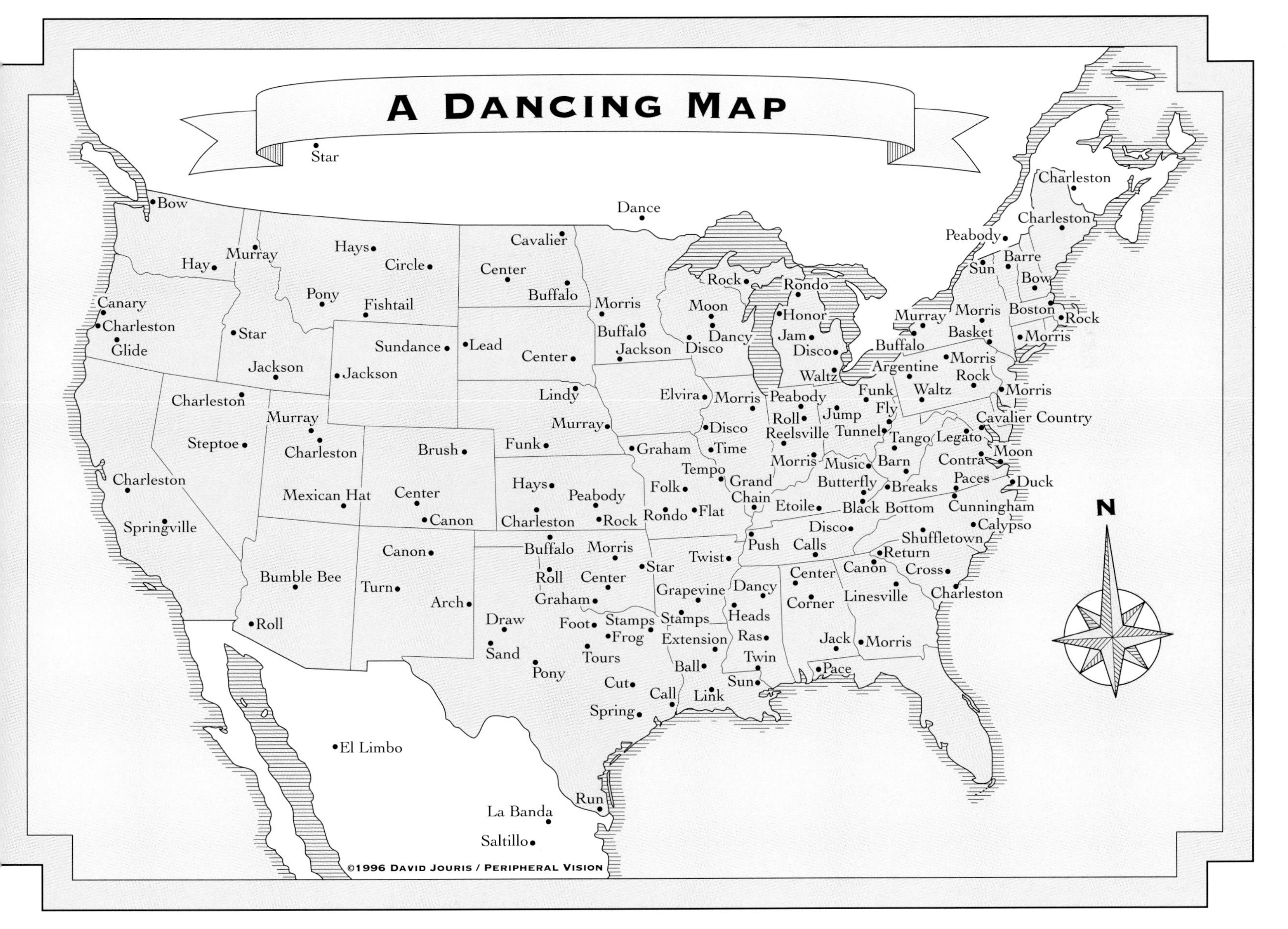
A DANCING MAP
Star
Bow
Dance
Cavalier
Hays
Murray
Hay
Circle
Center
Buffalo
Pony
Fishtail
Morris
Rock
Rondo
Canary
Charleston
Glide
Star
Sundance
Lead
Center
Buffalo
Jackson
Moon
Dancy
Disco
Honor
Jam
Disco
Waltz
Jackson
Jackson
Charleston
Lindy
Elvira
Morris
Peabody
Roll
Jump
Murray
Charleston
Steptoe
Murray
Funk
Disco
Time
Graham
Reelsville
Tunnel
Fly
Brush
Tempo
Morris
Music
Barn
Charleston
Hays
Peabody
Folk
Grand Chain
Butterfly
Breaks
Mexican Hat
Center
Canon
Charleston
Rock
Rondo
Flat
Etoile
Black Bottom
Springville
Canon
Buffalo
Morris
Star
Twist
Push
Calls
Disco
Bumble Bee
Turn
Roll
Center
Grapevine
Dancy
Center
Canon
Corner
Arch
Graham
Draw
Foot
Stamps
Stamps
Heads
Frog
Extension
Ras
Roll
Sand
Tours
Ball
Twin
Jack
Morris
Pace
Pony
Cut
Sun
Call
Link
Spring
El Limbo
Run
La Banda
Saltillo
Charleston
Charleston
Peabody
Sun
Barre
Bow
Murray
Morris
Boston
Rock
Basket
Morris
Buffalo
Argentine
Morris
Rock
Funk
Waltz
Morris
Cavalier Country
Tango
Legato
Moon
Contra
Duck
Paces
Cunningham
Calypso
Shuffletown
Return
Cross
Linesville
Charleston
N
©1996 DAVID JOURIS / PERIPHERAL VISION

The physician can bury his mistakes, but the architect can only advise his client to plant vines.
—Frank Lloyd Wright

The great thing about being an architect is you can walk into your dreams.
—Harold Wagoner

Lodgepole, NE, takes its name from Lodgepole Creek, which runs through the area. The creek's name is a translation of the original Dakota name, *tushu wakpala*. Native Americans found that the trees growing along the creek bank were suitable for cutting and using as lodgepoles for their shelters. By the way, about 100 miles away in Arthur, NE, there stands one of America's more unusual churches, built in the late 1920s—of straw. No longer used as a church (a building from Lodgepole was moved to Arthur to fill that need), it has been restored and is now a historic site open to the public.

Wikieup, AZ, uses an alternative spelling of *wickiup*, a Native American word meaning "dwelling." The town's name comes from Wikieup Canyon, where cowboys are said to have found ruins of a Hualapai Indian village. **House, NM**, however, isn't named for the form of shelter common to people living in this neighboring state, but for L. J. House, one of the early settlers and the community's first postmaster.

The name of **Interior, SD**, comes from its position in relation to the Badlands area. The town lies near the Badlands Wall, a sixty-mile-long spine of eroded terrain that stands 200 to 500 feet in height. **Wall, SD**, is also said to be named for this natural formation, although the town is more than eight miles away from the wall.

Located on the United States–Canadian border lies the aptly named **Portal, ND**. The town serves as an entrance way for both cars and trains headed to the province of Saskatchewan, Canada.

When its residents pitched in and built a small cottage for the widow of the late Methodist minister, the community took on the name of **Cottageville, SC**.

During World War II, prefabricated metal buildings, semicylindrical in shape, were used for troop shelters, warehouses, garages, machine shops, and even schools. Because these structures were designed by the U. S. Navy at Quonset Point, RI, the buildings were named Quonset huts.

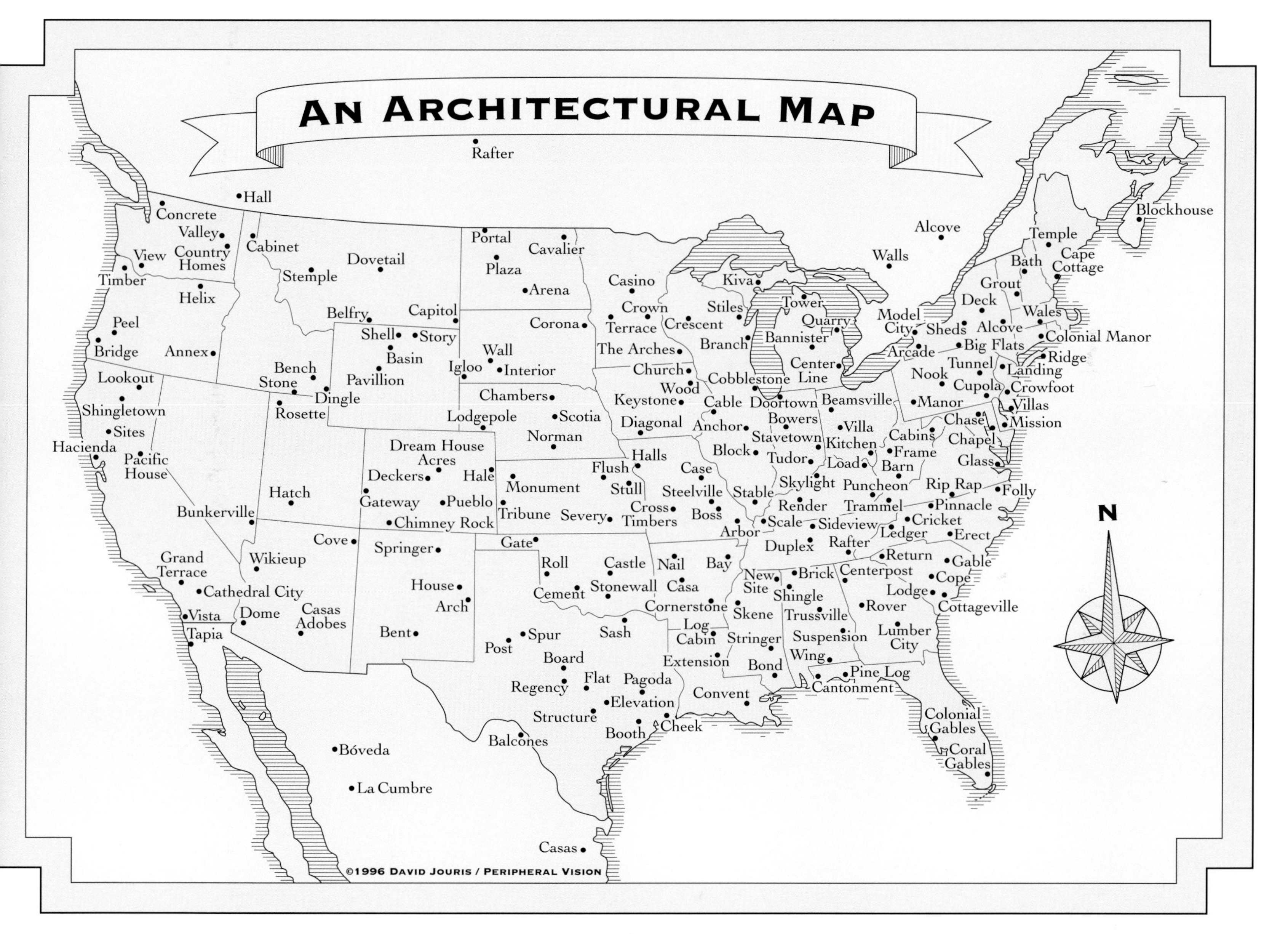
AN ARCHITECTURAL MAP
Rafter
Hall
Concrete
Valley
View
Country Homes
Timber
Cabinet
Helix
Stemple
Dovetail
Portal
Cavalier
Plaza
Arena
Casino
Crown
Terrace
Crescent
Kiva
Stiles
Tower
Quarry
Bannister
Branch
Alcove
Walls
Temple
Blockhouse
Bath
Cape Cottage
Grout
Deck
Wales
Model City
Sheds
Alcove
Colonial Manor
Big Flats
Ridge
Arcade
Tunnel
Landing
Nook
Cupola
Crowfoot
Manor
Villas
Chase
Mission
Peel
Bridge
Annex
Belfry
Capitol
Shell
Story
Basin
Wall
Interior
Igloo
Corona
The Arches
Church
Wood
Keystone
Cobblestone
Center Line
Cable
Doortown
Beamsville
Bench Stone
Pavillion
Dingle
Rosette
Lookout
Shingletown
Sites
Hacienda
Pacific House
Chambers
Scotia
Lodgepole
Norman
Diagonal
Anchor
Bowers
Villa
Stavetown
Kitchen
Cabins
Chapel
Block
Tudor
Load
Frame
Barn
Glass
Dream House Acres
Deckers
Hale
Monument
Halls
Flush
Stull
Case
Steelville
Stable
Skylight
Puncheon
Rip Rap
Folly
Hatch
Bunkerville
Gateway
Pueblo
Chimney Rock
Tribune
Severy
Cross Timbers
Boss
Render
Trammel
Pinnacle
Scale
Sideview
Cricket
Arbor
Ledger
Erect
Duplex
Rafter
Return
Gable
Cove
Springer
Gate
Roll
Castle
Nail
Bay
New Site
Brick
Centerpost
Cope
Lodge
Grand Terrace
Wikieup
Cathedral City
House
Cement
Stonewall
Casa
Shingle
Cottageville
Rover
Vista
Tapia
Dome
Casas Adobes
Arch
Cornerstone
Skene
Trussville
Bent
Spur
Post
Sash
Log Cabin
Stringer
Suspension
Lumber City
Board
Extension
Wing
Bond
Pine Log
Cantonment
Regency
Flat
Pagoda
Elevation
Convent
Structure
Cheek
Booth
Balcones
Colonial Gables
Coral Gables
Bóveda
La Cumbre
Casas
N
©1996 DAVID JOURIS / PERIPHERAL VISION

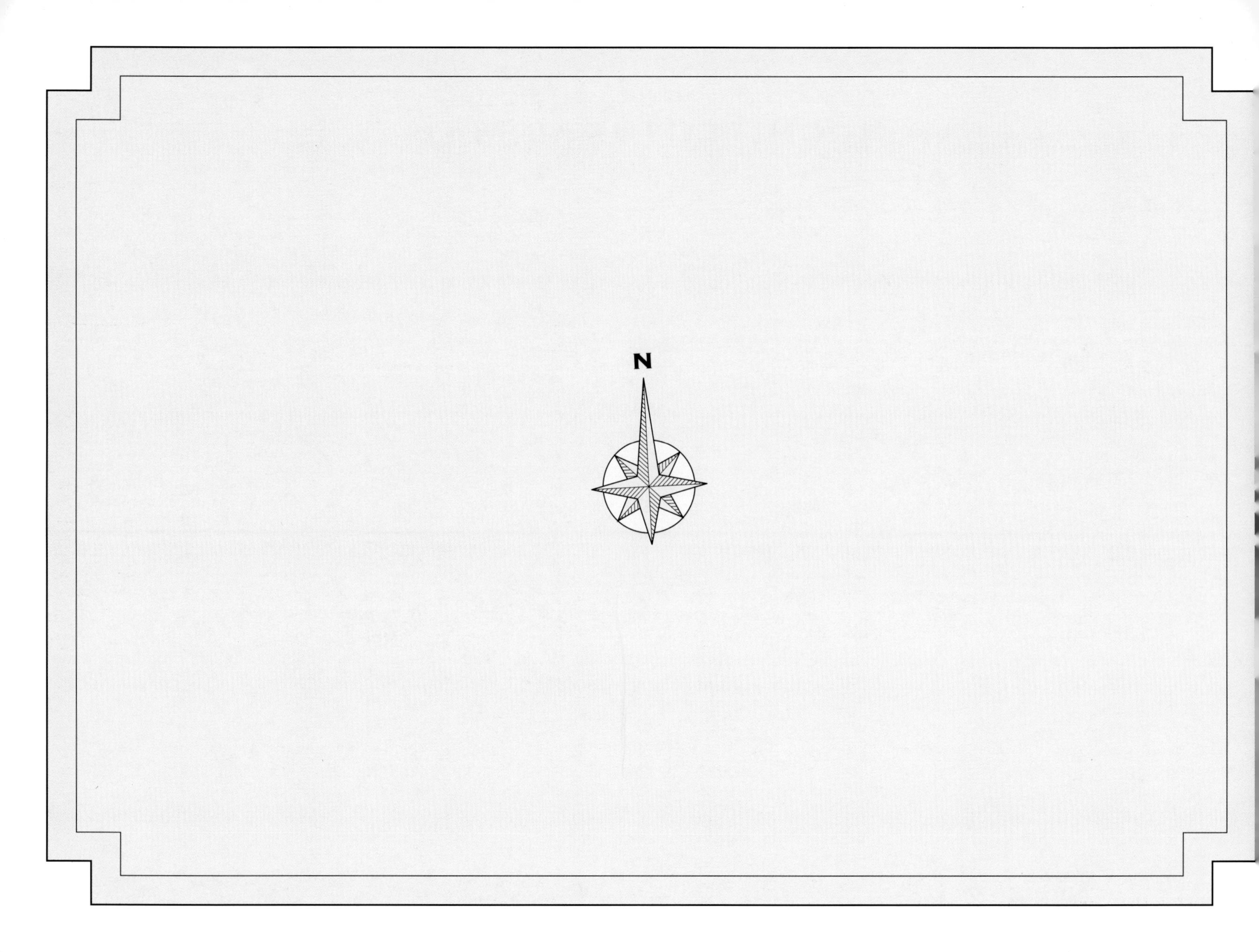
N

Ethnocentric Maps

Looking Out for Number One

What makes a nation in the beginning is a good piece of geography.
—ROBERT FROST

Patriotism is often an arbitrary veneration of real estate above principles.
—GEORGE JEAN NATHAN

Uncle Sam, LA, began as a plantation along the Mississippi River in the southwestern part of the state. The estate was built in 1836 by Mr. Samuel Fagot, known more familiarly to the locals as "Oncle Sam;"and before long the name was transferred to the plantation itself. Although the original buildings on the land have since been washed away into the river, the locale is still referred to as Uncle Sam.

Near Greenville, NH, stands the "Uncle Sam House," where Samuel Wilson, the original Uncle Sam, spent most of his first 40 years. In 1804 Wilson, long known as "Uncle Sam"—apparently a family trait, since his brother Edward was called "Uncle Ned," moved to Troy, NY, where he eventually contracted to supply the Army with meat during the War of 1812. His barrels were marked with the appropriate initials of the government: "U. S." It's said that one day a group of visitors commented on the large quantity of provisions awaiting shipment and asked what the initials stood for. A watchman employed by Wilson said that he didn't know, "...unless it means they belong to Uncle Sam." This idea spread rapidly and the usage of "Uncle Sam" to mean the "United States" appeared in newspapers by the following year.

During World War I, a number of American cities changed their names to avoid being associated with the enemy: Germantown, TX, became Shroeder, to honor a young soldier killed in battle against the Germans in 1918; Germantown, CA, changed its name to Artois, commemorating an embattled region in northwestern France; Germantown, KS, was renamed Mercier, after a Belgian religious leader; Potsdam, MO, changed its name to Pershing, in honor of the American general (whose ancestor had altered his name from the more Germanic-sounding Pfoersching); and Brandenburg, TX, changed its name to Old Glory. There was at least one attempt during WWI to pass a law prohibiting the delivery of mail to any municipality named Berlin or Germany but it was never made into law.

Now here's an amazing story: during World War II, gas was rationed and the ensuing difficulty in getting from one place to another made hitchhiking an acceptable—even patriotic—form of transportation. In September of 1943 an escaped convict from Ohio State Penitentiary named Ralph Schimpf was apprehended in Omaha, NE. Unfortunately, "due to transportation conditions," Ohio prison officials weren't able to retrieve their convict. A patriotic Schimpf volunteered to solve the problem by hitching back to Ohio. "We all got to do our bit at a time like this," he said. Amazingly, the police actually agreed to this idea; the escapee, true to his word, thumbed his way back to Columbus—and prison.

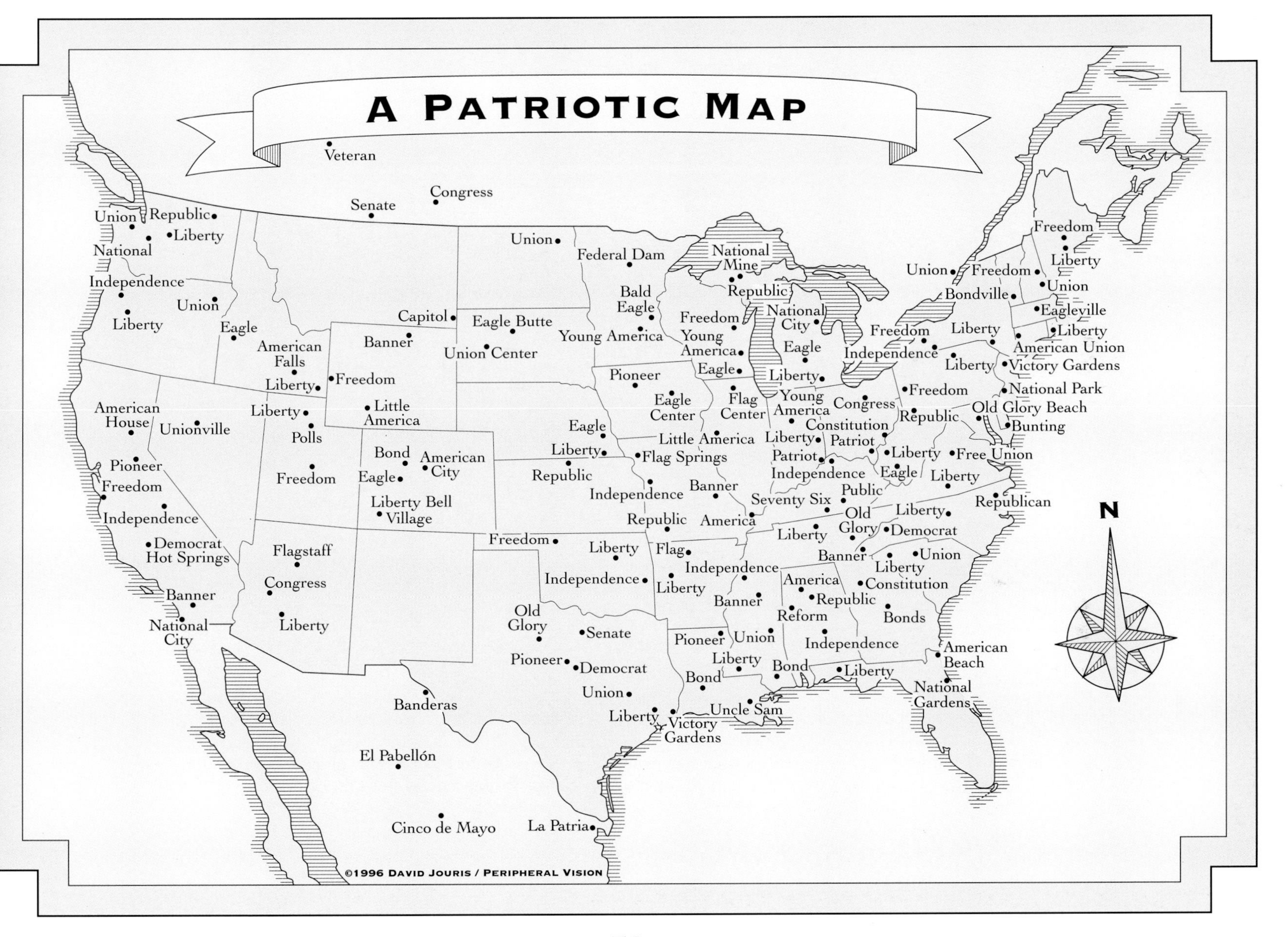
A PATRIOTIC MAP
Veteran
Congress
Senate
Union
Republic
Liberty
National
Independence
Union
Liberty
Eagle
Union
Federal Dam
National Mine
Republic
Bald Eagle
Capitol
Eagle Butte
Banner
American Falls
Union Center
Young America
Freedom
Young America
National City
Eagle
Freedom
Liberty
Independence
Freedom
Union
Freedom
Liberty
Union
Bondville
Eagleville
Liberty
American Union
Liberty
Victory Gardens
National Park
Old Glory Beach
Bunting
Liberty
Freedom
Pioneer
Eagle
Liberty
Flag Center
Eagle Center
Young America
Congress
Constitution
Freedom
Republic
American House
Unionville
Liberty
Little America
Polls
Eagle
Little America
Liberty
Patriot
Liberty
Free Union
Liberty
Flag Springs
Patriot
Independence
Eagle
Liberty
Bond
American City
Eagle
Republic
Pioneer
Freedom
Freedom
Independence
Banner
Public
Seventy Six
Old Glory
Republican
Liberty
Liberty Bell Village
Independence
Republic
America
Democrat
Hot Springs
Freedom
Liberty
Democrat
Liberty
Flagstaff
Flag
Banner
Union
Independence
Liberty
Congress
Independence
Liberty
America
Constitution
Banner
Republic
Banner
National City
Old Glory
Reform
Bonds
Liberty
Senate
Pioneer
Union
Independence
American Beach
Pioneer
Democrat
Liberty
Bond
Liberty
Bond
National Gardens
Union
Banderas
Uncle Sam
Liberty
Victory Gardens
El Pabellón
Cinco de Mayo
La Patria
©1996 DAVID JOURIS / PERIPHERAL VISION
N

New York is an exciting town where something is happening all the time—most of it unsolved.
—**Johnny Carson**

Our story begins, as all great stories do, in Brooklyn.
—**Jon Kalish**

The derivation of a number of New York's districts provides an interesting glimpse into the city's history. The Dutch influence is seen in names like Brooklyn (derived from the Dutch town *Breukelen*, meaning "swampy land"), Flushing (a corruption of the word *Vlissingen*, meaning "fortress on the water"), and Harlem (honoring the Dutch city of *Haarlem*—*haar* "height" + *lem* "clay"). Greenwich Village, once a distinct settlement on the island of Manhattan, is named after the English town of *Greenwich*. Greenwich means "green village," and thus Greenwich Village actually means "green village village." So nice, they named it twice?

The name of another English village, that of *Gotham*, was first used as a nickname for New York City by author Washington Irving. He found a similarity in the citizenry, referring to the reputation of the English villagers who were said to be "wise fools"—that is, "they appear hopelessly stupid, but for good reason." Further, the pseudonym that Irving employed in his book *History of New York*, Diedrich Knickerbocker, was taken as a synonym for a New Yorker. It is from this nickname that the city's professional basketball team—the Knicks—takes its name.

The good citizens of **Manhattan, KS**, home to only 33,000 people, have shown a kinship to their eastern cousin and its population of some eight million people by painting the words "The Little Apple" on the town water tower. One possible origin of the New York nickname of "The Big Apple" is the Spanish language. The Spanish word for a block of houses is *manzana*. One can see how the tall, densely inhabited districts of New York might be referred to as "The Big Blocks." The primary meaning of *manzana*, however, is "apple!"

William H. Bonney, better known as the outlaw Billy the Kid, was a New Yorker! He may have raised hell in the southwestern part of the country, but he wasn't born in **New York, NM**; he was actually a native of the Empire State, born not far from Hells Kitchen in 1859. Another New Yorker who wrought havoc—without leaving town—was Mary Mallon, a cook who infected dozens of New Yorkers with typhoid fever in the early 1900s. A carrier who was evidently immune to the disease herself, Typhoid Mary repeatedly broke her promises to keep out of kitchens; in desperation, health officials forcibly confined her to a hospital where she remained for the last twenty-three years of her life.

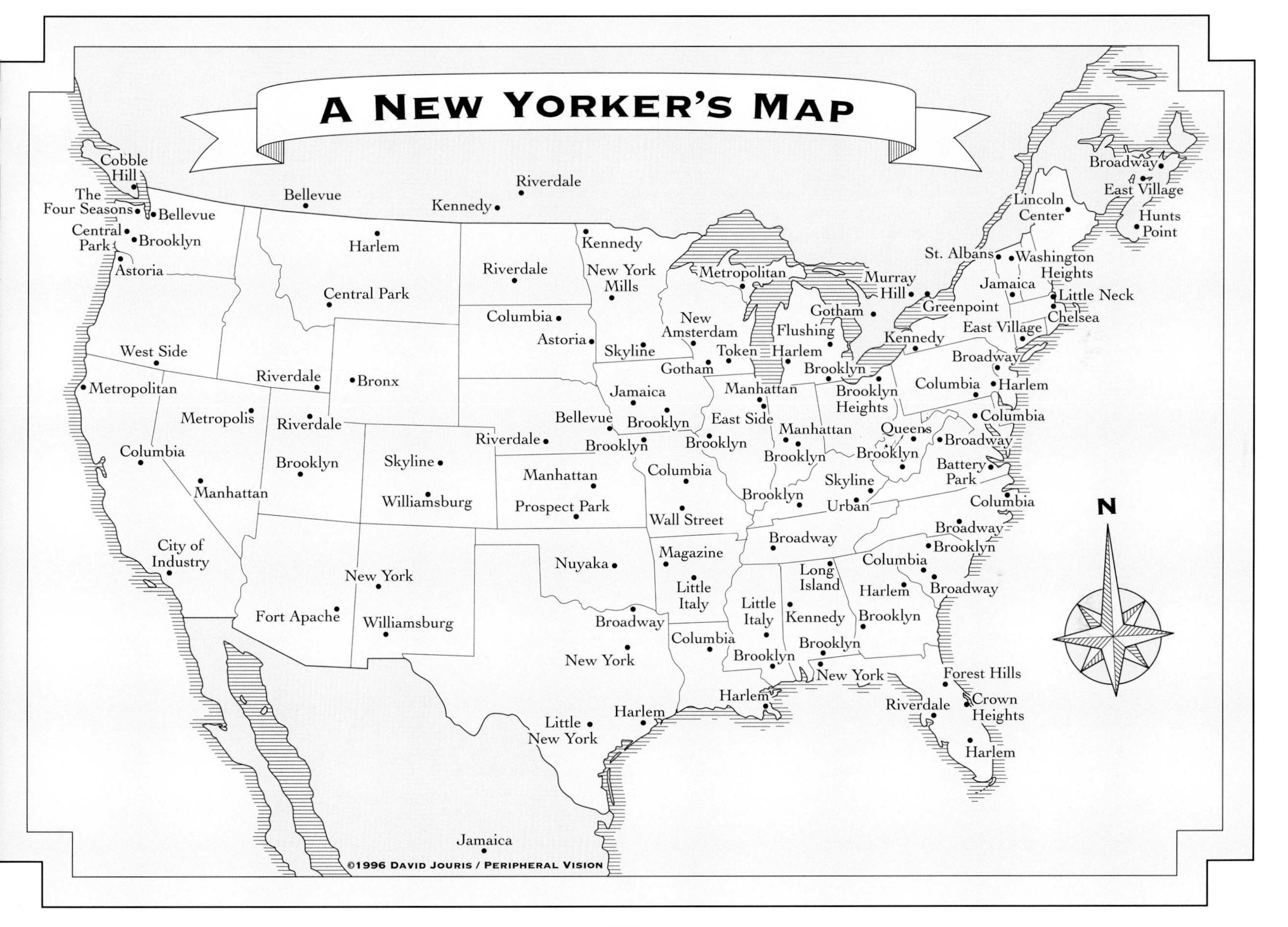
A NEW YORKER'S MAP
Cobble Hill
The Four Seasons
Bellevue
Central Park
Brooklyn
Astoria
Bellevue
Harlem
Riverdale
Kennedy
Riverdale
Kennedy
New York Mills
Central Park
Columbia
Astoria
West Side
Metropolitan
Metropolis
Riverdale
Bronx
Riverdale
Columbia
Manhattan
Brooklyn
Skyline
Williamsburg
Riverdale
Manhattan
Prospect Park
City of Industry
New York
Fort Apache
Williamsburg
Nuyaka
Broadway
New York
Little New York
Harlem
Jamaica
Metropolitan
New Amsterdam
Skyline
Token
Gotham
Jamaica
Bellevue
Brooklyn
Brooklyn
Columbia
Wall Street
Magazine
Little Italy
Columbia
Harlem
Gotham
Flushing
Harlem
Brooklyn
Manhattan
East Side
Brooklyn
Manhattan
Brooklyn
Brooklyn
Broadway
Little Italy
Brooklyn
Long Island
Kennedy
Brooklyn
New York
Murray Hill
Greenpoint
Kennedy
Brooklyn Heights
Queens
Brooklyn
Skyline
Urban
Columbia
Harlem
Brooklyn
Forest Hills
Riverdale
Crown Heights
Harlem
Broadway
East Village
Lincoln Center
Hunts Point
St. Albans
Washington Heights
Jamaica
Little Neck
Chelsea
East Village
Broadway
Columbia
Harlem
Columbia
Broadway
Battery Park
Columbia
Broadway
Brooklyn
Broadway
N
©1996 DAVID JOURIS / PERIPHERAL VISION

Californians are a race of people; they are not merely inhabitants of a State.
—O. Henry

The state motto, "Eureka" (meaning "I have found it"), seems as fitting for California today as it did a hundred and fifty years ago during the gold rush. (Legend has it that the Greek mathematician Archimedes uttered this famous word when thinking about gold, too.) These days, instead of referring to the discovery of gold, it seems to be the opinion of a great number of visitors to the Golden State—enamored of the splendid weather, the varied landscape, the availability of a wide array of fresh fruits and vegetables, and the wonderful diversity of cultures and ethnicities.

North Beach, MD, is not named after the original home of the beat generation in northern California, but because it is the northernmost beach in the county. The North Beach district of San Francisco is so named because it was at one time, earlier in the city's history, an actual beach. By the early 1960s, however, the beach had been moved out and in its place were beatniks—drinking coffee and writing poetry in the cafes. The fame of some of the beats has been acknowledged by their adopted city: there is a little alley in San Francisco named after Jack Kerouac; as well as Kenneth Rexroth Place and Via Ferlinghetti.

Evidently the word *pasadena*, meaning "between the hills" or "gap between mountains," originated in a Native American language—possibly Algonquin. The word was taken to California by fruit growers from the east who settled on the west coast. Some years later, several businessmen bought land in Maryland with the intention of raising silkworms there. The wife of one of these men chose the name Pasadena after her former home in California. Alas, in spite of the fact that the location lacks hills or mountains, the name proved more successful than the silkworms. Although **Pasadena, MD**, was named in honor of the southern California town that stages the Rose Bowl Parade each year, there is no floral procession in the east coast town. It seems, in fact, that their only community event is the annual Turtle Race, held in the library parking lot in mid July—which, given the speed of the animals involved, could last as long as the endless parade of floats on New Year's Day in California.

In 1923 a Texas real estate promoter named F. Z. Bishop bought some land that was formerly the Dull Ranch. Bishop was looking for a name that was more lively than, say, Dullsville. He decided on **Los Angeles, TX**, since he felt there was a similarity in climate with the sprawling southern California city. (The existence of this little Texas town makes it theoretically possible for one to claim that they can walk across Los Angeles in under an hour.)

California, PA, was founded in 1849, not long after word of the discovery of gold out west reached Pennsylvania. And, of course, the town was named for the Golden State.

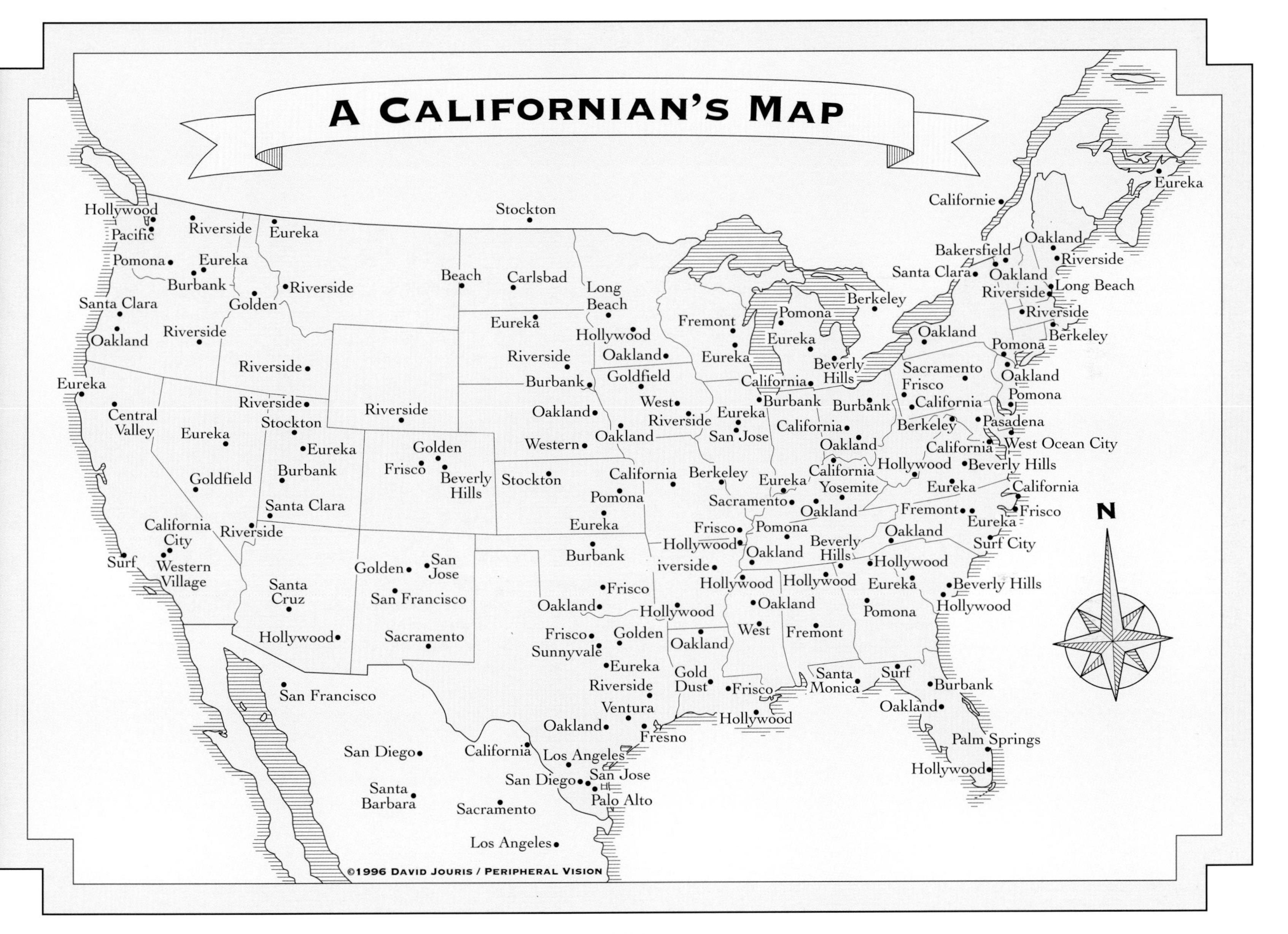
A CALIFORNIAN'S MAP
Hollywood
Pacific
Riverside
Eureka
Stockton
Pomona
Eureka
Burbank
Riverside
Golden
Beach
Carlsbad
Long Beach
Santa Clara
Oakland
Riverside
Eureka
Hollywood
Riverside
Oakland
Riverside
Goldfield
Burbank
Eureka
Central Valley
Riverside
Stockton
Riverside
Oakland
West
Riverside
Eureka
Eureka
Golden
Western
Oakland
Frisco
Beverly Hills
Stockton
Goldfield
Burbank
California
Pomona
Santa Clara
Eureka
California City
Riverside
Surf
Western Village
Golden
San Jose
Burbank
Santa Cruz
San Francisco
Frisco
Oakland
Hollywood
Hollywood
Sacramento
Frisco
Sunnyvale
Golden
Eureka
San Francisco
Riverside
Ventura
Oakland
Fresno
San Diego
California
Los Angeles
San Diego
San Jose
Palo Alto
Santa Barbara
Sacramento
Los Angeles
Fremont
Eureka
California
Burbank
Eureka
San Jose
Berkeley
Sacramento
Frisco
Hollywood
iverside
Hollywood
Oakland
Gold Dust
Frisco
Hollywood
Pomona
Eureka
Beverly Hills
Burbank
California
Oakland
California
Yosemite
Oakland
Pomona
Oakland
Beverly Hills
Hollywood
West
Fremont
Santa Monica
Berkeley
Oakland
Sacramento
Frisco
California
Berkeley
California
Hollywood
Eureka
Fremont
Oakland
Hollywood
Eureka
Pomona
Surf
Burbank
Oakland
Palm Springs
Hollywood
Californie
Bakersfield
Santa Clara
Oakland
Oakland
Riverside
Riverside
Long Beach
Riverside
Berkeley
Pomona
Oakland
Pomona
Pasadena
West Ocean City
Beverly Hills
California
Frisco
Eureka
Surf City
Beverly Hills
Hollywood
Eureka
N
©1996 DAVID JOURIS / PERIPHERAL VISION

Texas is a state of mind. Texas is an obsession. Above all, Texas is a nation in every sense of the word.

—John Steinbeck

You can always tell a Texan—but not much.

—Anonymous

Maverick, TX, is named for Samuel Maverick, who purchased land here in 1838. Sam Maverick wasn't a cattleman, merely a landowner who was given several hundred cattle as payment for a debt. The ranch hand in charge of Maverick's land, having better things to do than brand all these cattle, let them wander the range unmarked. Aware of this, the neighboring ranchers began referring to all unbranded cattle as "Maverick's." The term spread widely, and eventually *maverick* came to mean not only cattle that strayed, but a person who strayed from conventional beliefs. The Maverick family also gave another word to the language—*gobbledygook*—which was coined by Samuel Maverick's grandson Maury, who was attempting to combat "wordy and generally unintelligible jargon" that he found so rampant where he worked. Not surprisingly, he was serving in Congress at the time.

Houston, MO, is named for the famous Texan whose name is also honored, of course, by a Lone Star State metropolis. (Incidently, the Missouri town is located in Texas County—so named because it is the largest county in the state.) Sam Houston, a native of Virginia, was commander of the troops of the provincial Texan government in their fight against the Mexican army. When Texas became a republic, Houston became its first president; later, when Texas joined the Union, Houston became a senator and eventually served as governor of the state. He was soon forced to leave office, however, because of his opposition to the Confederacy. By the way, historians have pointed out that one of the main reasons Mexican General Santa Anna lost the Battle of San Jacinto (near present-day Houston, TX)—and hence all of Texas—was because instead of commanding his troops he was dallying with a mulatto slave girl named Emily Morgan. Later, a famous song was written in honor of this young woman ("the sweetest rose of color"): "The Yellow Rose of Texas."

The name Texas is derived from the word *Tejas,* understood by Spanish explorers to indicate the Native Americans who lived in the region (centered in East Texas and Louisiana). Actually, the Indians were a confederacy called the Hasinai, and the word *tejas* simply meant "friends" or "allies." This concept is reflected in the Texas state motto: Friendship.

Texas is called the Lone Star State because there is a single star in the state flag, held over from the time when it served as the flag of the Republic of Texas. Since the influx of Europeans, there have been six flags over Texas—those of Spain, France, Mexico, the Republic of Texas, the Confederacy, and the United States.

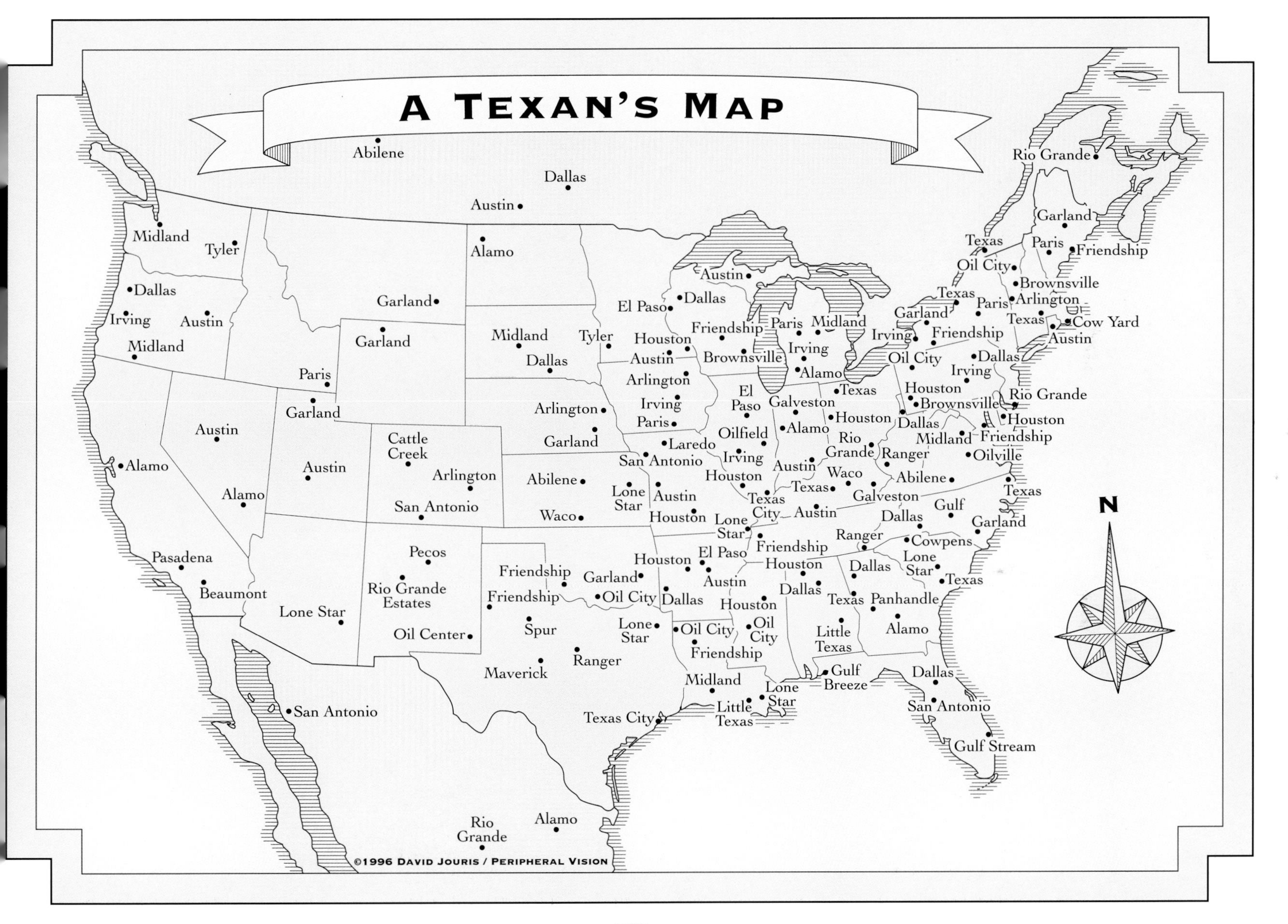
A TEXAN'S MAP
Abilene
Dallas
Austin
Alamo
Midland
Tyler
Dallas
Irving
Austin
Midland
Garland
Garland
Paris
Garland
Austin
Austin
Alamo
Alamo
Cattle Creek
Arlington
San Antonio
Midland
Dallas
Tyler
Arlington
Garland
Abilene
Waco
Pasadena
Beaumont
Lone Star
Pecos
Rio Grande Estates
Oil Center
Friendship
Friendship
Spur
Maverick
Ranger
Garland
Oil City
San Antonio
Rio Grande
Alamo
El Paso
Dallas
Austin
Houston
Austin
Arlington
Irving
Paris
Laredo
San Antonio
Lone Star
Austin
Houston
Houston
Austin
Dallas
Lone Star
Oil City
Friendship
Midland
Texas City
Little Texas
Lone Star
Friendship
Brownsville
Paris
Midland
Irving
Alamo
El Paso
Galveston
Texas
Alamo
Houston
Oilfield
Irving
Houston
Rio Grande
Austin
Waco
Texas
Texas City
Lone Star
Austin
El Paso
Friendship
Houston
Houston
Dallas
Oil City
Little Texas
Gulf Breeze
Rio Grande
Garland
Texas
Paris
Friendship
Oil City
Brownsville
Texas
Paris
Arlington
Texas
Cow Yard
Austin
Garland
Irving
Friendship
Oil City
Dallas
Irving
Houston
Brownsville
Rio Grande
Dallas
Houston
Midland
Friendship
Ranger
Oilville
Abilene
Galveston
Texas
Gulf
Dallas
Garland
Ranger
Cowpens
Lone Star
Dallas
Texas
Texas
Panhandle
Alamo
Dallas
San Antonio
Gulf Stream
N

N

FAMOUS MAPS

The Name Game

Very few things happen at the right time, and the rest do not happen at all; the conscientious historian will correct these defects.

—HERODOTUS

History is all explained by geography.

—ROBERT PENN WARREN

Hiawatha, UT, took its name from the popular Henry Wadsworth Longfellow poem, "The Song of Hiawatha." Longfellow himself took this name from the legendary Native American leader who is credited with helping to found the Iroquois Confederacy in the 1500s.

Marion is a town name found throughout the southeast to commemorate Francis Marion, a Revolutionary War hero known as the Swamp Fox. Marion's popularity was a direct result of a biography published by the inimitable "Parson" Weems in 1809. **Marion, SC**, is located in Marion County, just north of the area where the Swamp Fox waged a number of campaigns against the British.

Earp, CA, was named for Wyatt Earp shortly after his death in 1928. Earp had come to prospect in this desert area in the early 1900s and, after hitting paydirt, mined there off and on during the last twenty years of his life. Earp is best known for having been a lawman in Tombstone, AZ, "the town too tough to die."

Named after the daughter of a Powhatan chief, **Pocahontas, AR**, honors the young woman who interceded to save the life of Englishman John Smith. The name was chosen because the town was first populated by a number of settlers from Virginia, where the Powhatan tribe lived.

Geronimo, a Chiricahua Apache, led the last major armed resistance by Indians in the southwest. When he surrendered in Arizona in 1886, Geronimo was sent to Fort Sill, OK, where he lived out the remaining twenty years of his life as a prisoner of war. **Geronimo, OK**, just south of Fort Sill, honors the great Apache chief. The name Geronimo is actually Spanish for Jerome; the famed warrior's real name was Goyahkla—"one who yawns"—perhaps a more fitting name for this sleepy little Oklahoma town of fewer than 800 people.

When the Mississippi towns of Garley and Ebenezer decided to merge, the residents could not agree on what they should call the resulting community. It was finally suggested by one participant that they name the place **Bunker Hill, MS**, since there was such a battle over it. And so they did. (Let's not go into the question of whether or not the actual Battle of Bunker Hill was really fought on nearby Breed's Hill.)

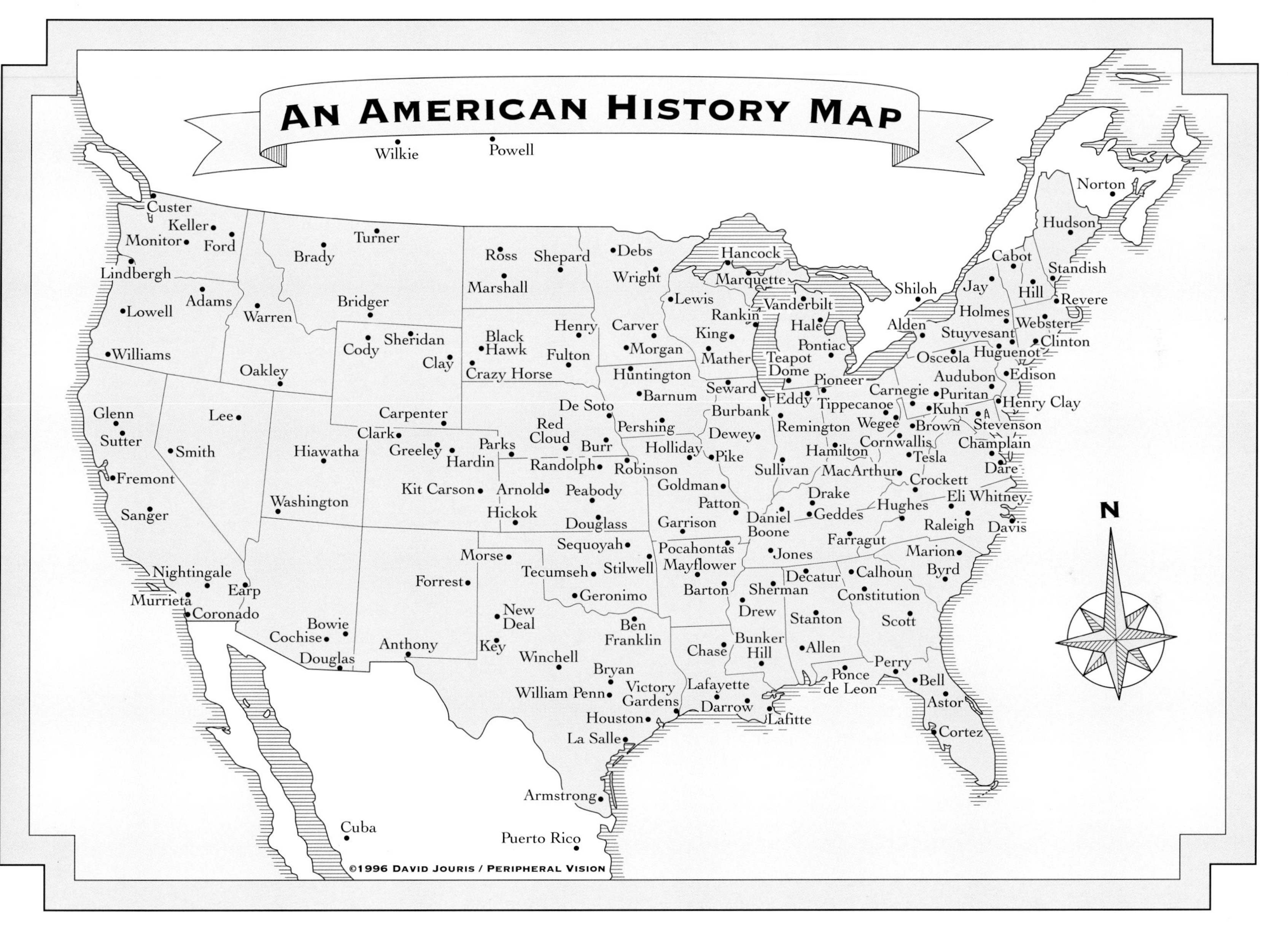
AN AMERICAN HISTORY MAP
Wilkie
Powell
Norton
Custer
Keller
Ford
Monitor
Turner
Brady
Ross
Shepard
Debs
Hancock
Hudson
Lindbergh
Wright
Marquette
Cabot
Standish
Adams
Marshall
Shiloh
Jay
Hill
Lowell
Warren
Bridger
Lewis
Vanderbilt
Revere
Rankin
Holmes
Henry
Carver
Hale
Alden
Webster
Black Hawk
King
Stuyvesant
Cody
Sheridan
Pontiac
Clinton
Williams
Clay
Morgan
Fulton
Mather
Teapot Dome
Osceola
Huguenot
Oakley
Crazy Horse
Huntington
Audubon
Edison
Pioneer
Seward
Carnegie
Puritan
Barnum
Eddy
De Soto
Tippecanoe
Henry Clay
Glenn
Carpenter
Burbank
Kuhn
Lee
Red Cloud
Pershing
Wegee
Brown
Stevenson
Remington
Sutter
Clark
Dewey
Cornwallis
Champlain
Parks
Burr
Hiawatha
Greeley
Holliday
Hamilton
Smith
Pike
Tesla
Hardin
Randolph
Robinson
Sullivan
MacArthur
Dare
Fremont
Crockett
Goldman
Kit Carson
Arnold
Peabody
Drake
Eli Whitney
Washington
Patton
Hughes
Hickok
Geddes
Sanger
Daniel Boone
Raleigh
Garrison
Douglass
Davis
Farragut
Sequoyah
Pocahontas
Morse
Jones
Marion
Mayflower
Stilwell
Tecumseh
Calhoun
Byrd
Nightingale
Decatur
Forrest
Earp
Sherman
Barton
Constitution
Murrieta
Geronimo
Coronado
New Deal
Drew
Stanton
Scott
Ben Franklin
Bowie
Cochise
Bunker Hill
Key
Anthony
Chase
Allen
Douglas
Winchell
Perry
Bryan
Ponce de Leon
Bell
Victory Gardens
Lafayette
William Penn
Astor
Darrow
Houston
Lafitte
La Salle
Cortez
Armstrong
Cuba
Puerto Rico
©1996 DAVID JOURIS / PERIPHERAL VISION
N

He thought he was the King of America
Where they pour Coca Cola just like vintage wine.
—**ELVIS COSTELLO**, "Brilliant Mistake"

This one's for you, Rex.
—**LOUIS ARMSTRONG**, *to King George VI during a command performance.*

Kingsville, TX, established in 1904, is located in the heart of land owned by the King Ranch, an enterprise spreading through seven counties in the southern part of Texas between Corpus Christi and the Mexican border. This ranch—the largest cattle empire in the world, with 1.25 million acres—began when riverboat captain Richard King purchased a Spanish land grant of 75,000 acres in Nueces County in 1852. Among other things, the ranch is known for its quarter-horses and for developing a new breed of cattle that is a cross between the shorthorn and the Brahman.

Kingdom City, MO, seems to have gotten its name due to two coinciding facts. The name was proposed by the founders of the Kingdom Oil Company. The name found favor with the residents because the community took great pride in a legendary Civil War incident whereby a rag-tag group of Calloway County boys and old men managed to fool a Union force of some 500 well-trained troops into signing a nonaggression pact. Locals later took to refering to the county as the independent Kingdom of Callaway.

The farming community of **Ras, MS**, takes its name from Ras Reed, a lifelong resident. Mr. Reed was a very well-liked and honorable fellow—a prince among men. Interestingly enough, "Ras" is the Ethiopian title for a royal prince. Before he succeeded to the throne in Ethiopia, Emperor Haile Selassie was called Ras Tafari, and it is from him that the sect members called Rastafarians take their name.

The United States has actually had an emperor of its own. Joshua Norton, an Englishman raised in South Africa, eventually emigrated to San Francisco where he settled in the mid 1800s. In a failed attempt to corner the rice market, Norton lost everything—including his grip on reality. Proclaiming himself Emperor of the United States and Protector of Mexico, Norton I wore a regal costume, issued decrees, and imposed taxes on local businessmen. (Even then the good citizens of San Francisco seemed to take eccentricity in stride.) At one point, Norton I issued an edict making it a High Misdemeanor, punishable by a stiff fine, to "utter the abominable word 'Frisco.'" This nickname, still unwelcome in the city, began as the code written on railroad freight to designate it was bound for San Francisco.

Trivia lovers might appreciate the fact that **Queensport, Nova Scotia**, in Canada, has the honor of being the shortest town name in the world containing eight consecutive letters of the alphabet (from N through U—although not in that order!).

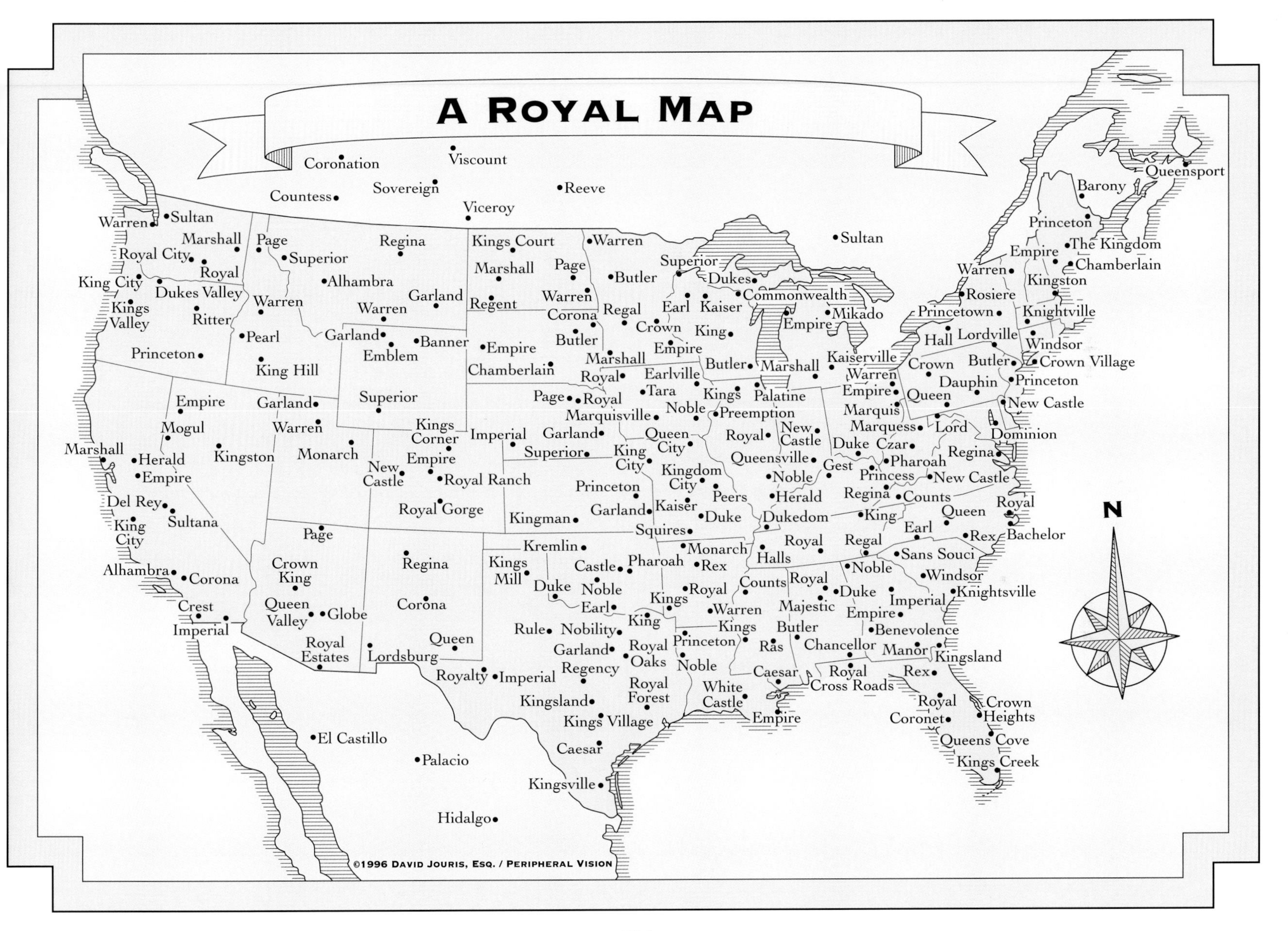
A ROYAL MAP
Coronation
Viscount
Countess
Sovereign
Reeve
Viceroy
Barony
Queensport
Warren
Sultan
Marshall
Page
Superior
Regina
Kings Court
Warren
Sultan
Princeton
The Kingdom
Royal City
Royal
King City
Dukes Valley
Alhambra
Marshall
Page
Butler
Superior
Dukes
Empire
Chamberlain
Warren
Kingston
Kings Valley
Ritter
Warren
Garland
Warren
Regent
Warren
Corona
Regal
Earl
Kaiser
Commonwealth
Mikado
Empire
Rosiere
Princetown
Knightville
Pearl
Garland
Banner
Emblem
Empire
Butler
Crown
King
Empire
Hall
Lordville
Windsor
Princeton
King Hill
Marshall
Chamberlain
Royal
Earlville
Butler
Marshall
Kaiserville
Crown
Butler
Crown Village
Warren
Dauphin
Princeton
Empire
Garland
Superior
Page
Royal
Tara
Kings
Palatine
Empire
Queen
New Castle
Mogul
Warren
Kings Corner
Marquisville
Noble
Preemption
Marquis
Lord
Marquess
Dominion
Marshall
Herald
Empire
Kingston
Monarch
Imperial
Garland
Queen City
Royal
New Castle
Duke
Czar
Regina
Superior
King City
Queensville
Gest
Pharoah
New Castle
Empire
Royal Ranch
Kingdom City
Noble
Princess
Princeton
Peers
Herald
Regina
Counts
Del Rey
Sultana
Royal Gorge
Garland
Kaiser
Duke
Dukedom
King
Queen
Royal
King City
Kingman
Squires
Earl
Rex
Bachelor
Page
Kremlin
Monarch
Royal
Regal
Sans Souci
Crown King
Regina
Kings Mill
Castle
Pharoah
Rex
Halls
Noble
Alhambra
Corona
Duke
Noble
Counts
Royal
Duke
Windsor
Knightsville
Royal
Kings
Imperial
Crest
Queen Valley
Globe
Corona
Earl
Warren
Majestic
Empire
Imperial
King
Kings
Butler
Benevolence
Rule
Nobility
Royal Oaks
Princeton
Ras
Chancellor
Manor
Kingsland
Royal Estates
Lordsburg
Queen
Garland
Noble
Caesar
Royal Cross Roads
Rex
Royalty
Imperial
Regency
Royal Forest
White Castle
Royal
Crown Heights
Kingsland
Empire
Coronet
Kings Village
El Castillo
Palacio
Caesar
Queens Cove
Kings Creek
Kingsville
Hidalgo
N
©1996 DAVID JOURIS, ESQ. / PERIPHERAL VISION

The remarkable thing about Shakespeare is that he really is very good,
in spite of all the people who say he is very good.
—**ROBERT GRAVES**

I know not, sir, whether Bacon wrote the words of Shakespeare,
but if he did not, it seems to me he missed the opportunity of his life.
—**JAMES BARRIE**

If the truth be known, **Othello, WA**, originally had no relation to Shakespeare. Rather it was named at the beginning of the twentieth century by an early settler, Nettie Belle Chavis, for her childhood hometown (no longer in existence) in Tennessee. Many years later, however, a developer gave the town a Shakespearean flavor by choosing street names like Macbeth, Venice, Desdemona, and Hamlet. Coincidently, at one time there was also a post office named Hamlet located in this area.

Iago, TX, is said to be named for the character in William Shakespeare's *Othello*, although why the town would have chosen the name of the villain seems without rhyme or reason.

Given that there is a Rosalind Street in the city of **Orlando, FL**, one might feel pretty confident that the town is named after the character in *As You Like It*. Be that as it may, the city is actually named for Orlando Reeves, a soldier who was killed there long ago.

Although the name Rialto is mentioned in *The Merchant of Venice*, **Rialto, CA**, isn't named with reference to the Bard of Avon. There is a possibility that a settler's daughter got the name from the bridge spanning the Grand Canal in Venice, Italy, but it is also quite possible that the town's name comes from a contraction of the Spanish words *rio* + *alto*, meaning "high river."

Romeo, MI, was indeed named for the famous star-crossed lover. **Romeo, CO**, however, was originally named Romero after an early settler. As luck would have it, the postal authorities were having difficulties with what they felt were a surfeit of towns named Romero; they solved the problem by dropping the last consonant.

The town of **Banquo, IN**, was formerly named Priceville. It is rumored that a local supernatural legend inspired the town to rename itself after the ghost in Shakespeare's *Macbeth*.

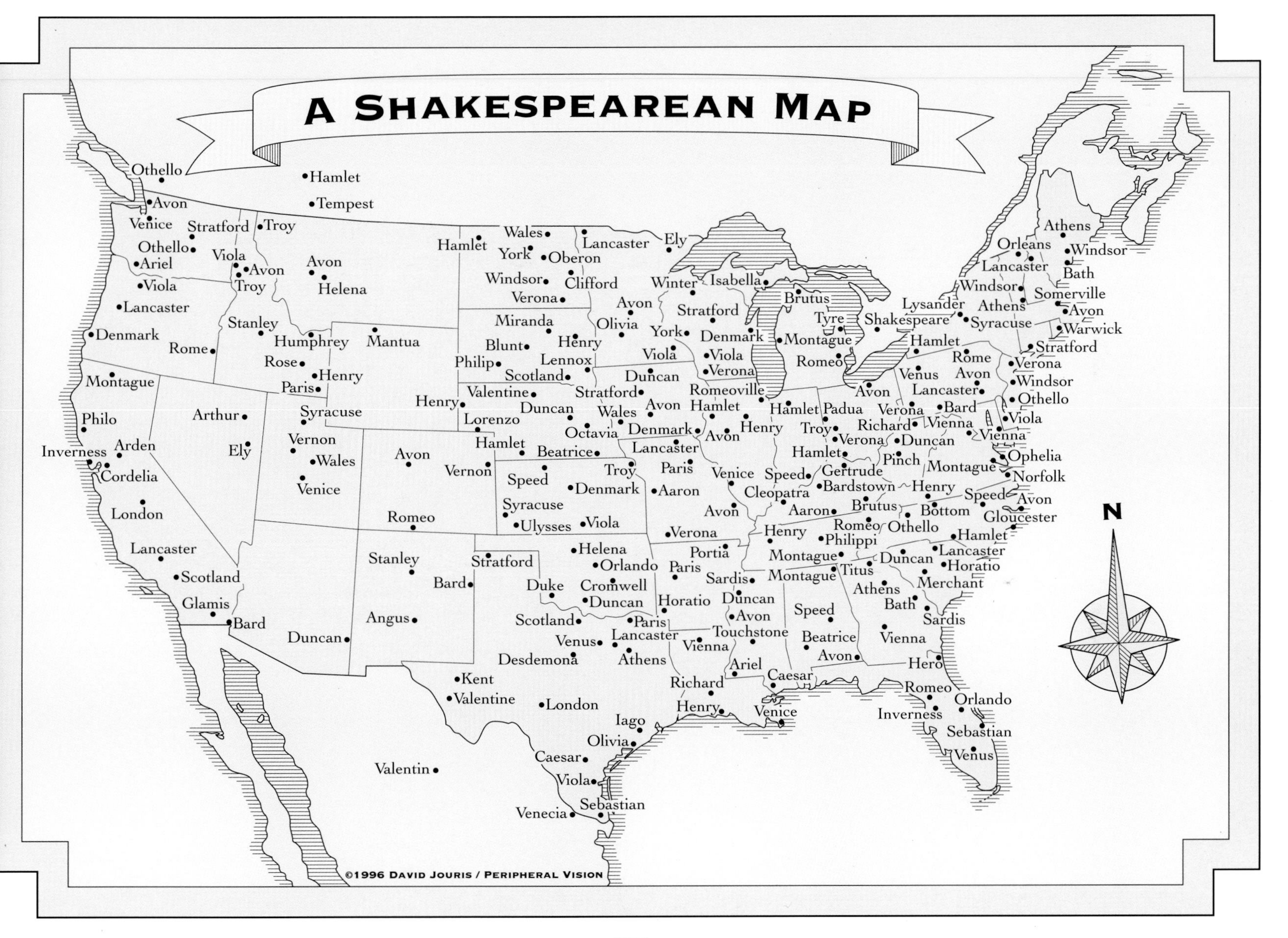

A SHAKESPEAREAN MAP
Othello
Hamlet
Avon
Tempest
Venice
Stratford
Troy
Othello
Viola
Ariel
Avon
Avon
Troy
Helena
Viola
Lancaster
Denmark
Stanley
Rome
Humphrey
Mantua
Rose
Henry
Montague
Paris
Syracuse
Philo
Arthur
Vernon
Arden
Inverness
Ely
Wales
Cordelia
Venice
Avon
London
Lancaster
Scotland
Glamis
Bard
Duncan
Angus
Stanley
Bard
Romeo
Hamlet
Wales
Lancaster
Ely
York
Oberon
Windsor
Clifford
Verona
Winter
Isabella
Avon
Miranda
Olivia
Stratford
Brutus
York
Blunt
Henry
Denmark
Tyre
Montague
Shakespeare
Lysander
Philip
Lennox
Viola
Viola
Romeo
Scotland
Duncan
Verona
Valentine
Stratford
Romeoville
Henry
Duncan
Wales
Avon
Hamlet
Hamlet
Padua
Lorenzo
Octavia
Denmark
Henry
Troy
Avon
Hamlet
Lancaster
Beatrice
Verona
Hamlet
Vernon
Troy
Paris
Venice
Speed
Gertrude
Speed
Denmark
Aaron
Cleopatra
Bardstown
Syracuse
Avon
Aaron
Brutus
Ulysses
Viola
Verona
Henry
Romeo
Othello
Philippi
Helena
Portia
Montague
Stratford
Orlando
Paris
Sardis
Montague
Titus
Duke
Cromwell
Duncan
Duncan
Horatio
Avon
Speed
Scotland
Paris
Touchstone
Venus
Lancaster
Vienna
Beatrice
Desdemona
Athens
Avon
Ariel
Caesar
Kent
Valentine
Richard
London
Henry
Venice
Iago
Olivia
Caesar
Valentin
Viola
Sebastian
Venecia
Athens
Orleans
Windsor
Lancaster
Bath
Windsor
Somerville
Athens
Avon
Syracuse
Warwick
Hamlet
Stratford
Rome
Verona
Venus
Avon
Windsor
Avon
Lancaster
Othello
Verona
Bard
Richard
Vienna
Viola
Verona
Duncan
Vienna
Pinch
Ophelia
Montague
Norfolk
Henry
Speed
Avon
Bottom
Gloucester
Hamlet
Lancaster
Duncan
Horatio
Merchant
Athens
Bath
Sardis
Vienna
Hero
Romeo
Orlando
Inverness
Sebastian
Venus
N
©1996 DAVID JOURIS / PERIPHERAL VISION

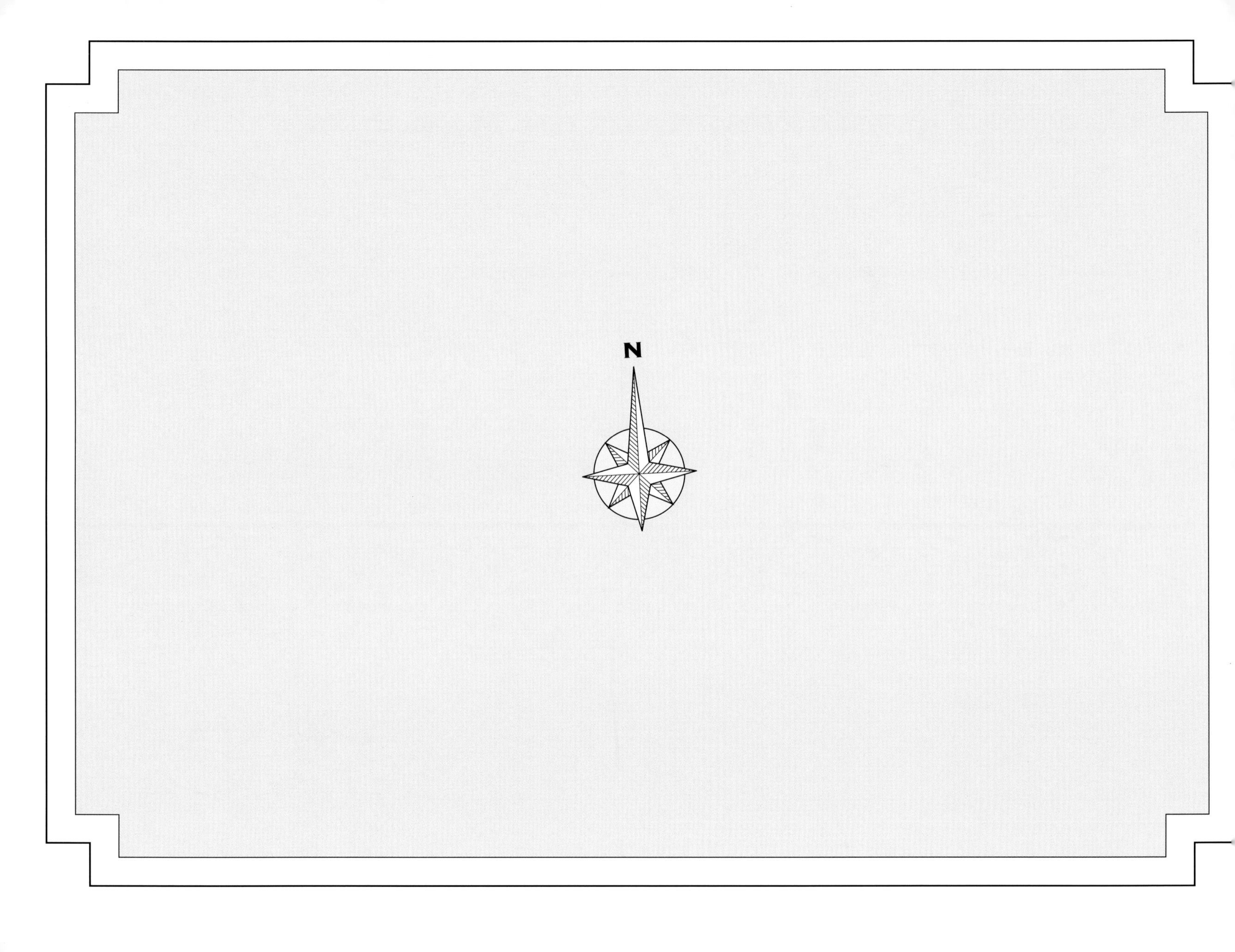
N

MILITANT MAPS

Maps You'll Need a Permit to Carry

Maps are one of the casualties of war,
the single purpose of which is to rewrite them.
—**Paul Theroux**

They couldn't hit an elephant at this dist—
—Last words of **General John Sedgwick**, *spoken as he looked towards enemy lines during the Civil War Battle of Spotsylvania Courthouse*

Battle Creek, MI, was originally the name given to a creek where an argument took place between members of a surveying party and a few Native Americans. The argument apparently grew into a "battle" in the retelling. When looking for a name for their village, the residents also considered an Indian name, *Waupakisko*, meaning "river of blood," probably referring to a more violent disagreement between two tribes in the area. Kellogg's and Post cereals both began life here, and a number of other cereal companies have come to the area, too—all battling for dominance at the breakfast table.

Nitro, WV, was established during World War I as a site for producing smokeless gunpowder via a nitrocellulose process from which the town's name derives. However, by the time the manufacturing plant was up and ready for production, the war was over. To make use of the new plant and equipment, and the large quantities of cotton that were rapidly piling up, an industry was developed that uses cellulose to manufacture its product: rayon.

Dragoon, AZ, was named for the 3rd U. S. Cavalry, stationed in the area during the mid to late 1800s. Commonly called the Dragoons, these soldiers were involved in many skirmishes with the Apaches in the southwest.

The small town of **Soldier, KS**, reflects the terrible fighting experienced by soldiers in the state of Kansas during the Civil War. The good citizens of Kansas didn't wait for war before they started fighting, however. By the time statehood arrived in early 1861, just before the war broke out, Kansas was already known as Bleeding Kansas due to the violence of both free and pro-slavery factions.

Although it isn't well known, Japanese incendiary devices and fragmentation bombs hit the U. S. mainland during World War II. Attached to paper balloons, they rode air currents for over five thousand miles before landing. (One made it almost as far as Detroit!) Of the thousands that were launched, only a small number worked as intended, producing mostly minimal property damage. One, for example, hit the main transmission lines in Hanford, WA (ironically, the site where plutonium for the Nagasaki bomb was being produced). The single incident involving human casualties occurred when a device was detonated by a child on Oregon's Gearhart Mountain in 1945—killing several children and a pregnant woman.

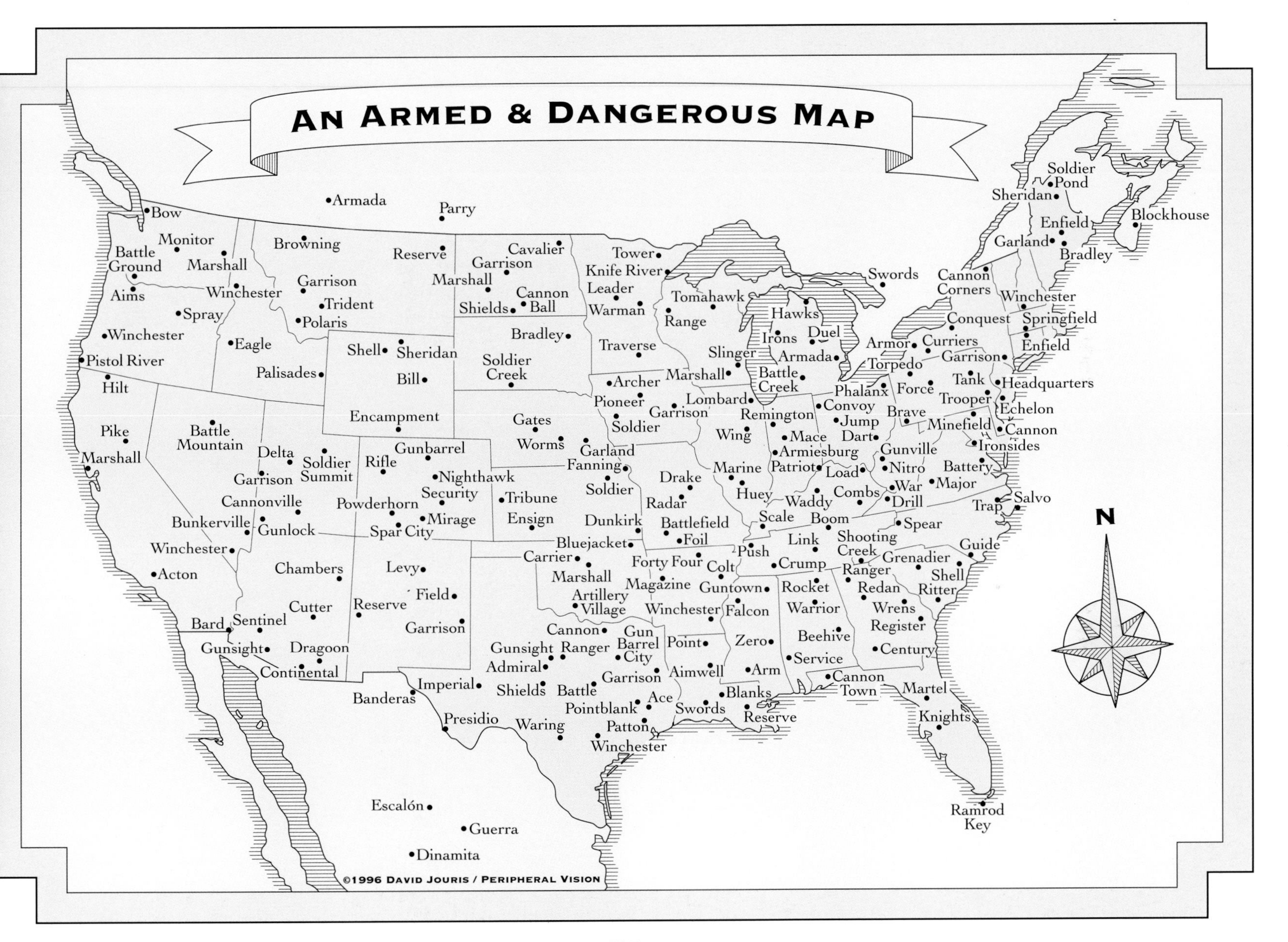
AN ARMED & DANGEROUS MAP
Bow
Armada
Parry
Battle Ground
Monitor
Marshall
Browning
Reserve
Cavalier
Garrison
Tower
Knife River
Leader
Warman
Aims
Winchester
Garrison
Marshall
Trident
Cannon Ball
Shields
Spray
Polaris
Winchester
Eagle
Shell
Sheridan
Bradley
Soldier Creek
Traverse
Tomahawk
Range
Hawks
Irons
Duel
Slinger
Armada
Marshall
Archer
Pistol River
Hilt
Palisades
Bill
Battle Creek
Lombard
Pioneer
Garrison
Soldier
Remington
Encampment
Gates
Worms
Garland
Fanning
Pike
Battle Mountain
Marshall
Delta
Soldier Summit
Rifle
Gunbarrel
Nighthawk
Security
Garrison
Cannonville
Powderhorn
Tribune
Mirage
Ensign
Soldier
Drake
Radar
Dunkirk
Battlefield
Foil
Bunkerville
Gunlock
Spar City
Bluejacket
Winchester
Acton
Chambers
Levy
Carrier
Marshall
Forty Four
Colt
Push
Crump
Magazine
Guntown
Field
Artillery Village
Winchester
Falcon
Cutter
Reserve
Garrison
Bard
Sentinel
Gunsight
Dragoon
Continental
Cannon
Gunsight
Ranger
Gun Barrel City
Point
Zero
Admiral
Garrison
Aimwell
Arm
Imperial
Shields
Battle
Ace
Pointblank
Swords
Blanks
Reserve
Banderas
Presidio
Waring
Patton
Winchester
Escalón
Guerra
Dinamita
Wing
Mace
Armiesburg
Marine
Patriot
Load
Huey
Waddy
Combs
Scale
Boom
Link
Shooting Creek
Rocket
Warrior
Beehive
Service
Cannon Town
Convoy
Jump
Dart
Phalanx
Torpedo
Armor
Curriers
Garrison
Force
Tank
Trooper
Brave
Minefield
Gunville
Nitro
War
Drill
Battery
Major
Spear
Grenadier
Ranger
Redan
Wrens
Register
Century
Martel
Knights
Ramrod Key
Shell
Ritter
Guide
Trap
Salvo
Ironsides
Cannon
Echelon
Headquarters
Swords
Cannon Corners
Conquest
Winchester
Springfield
Enfield
Soldier Pond
Sheridan
Enfield
Garland
Bradley
Blockhouse
N
©1996 DAVID JOURIS / PERIPHERAL VISION

Hold the fort! I am coming!
—**William Tecumseh Sherman**, *in a message to General John Corse, battle at Altoona, GA, in 1864.*

Back in the 1660s, King Charles II of England, for reasons best known only to himself, gave the same tract of land to both Connecticut and Pennsylvania. A hundred years later, the Colony of Connecticut decided to take possession of the land that it had been granted. Forty men from Connecticut, sent to hold the land against any claim by either the Native Americans or the Pennsylvanians, built a fort on the site of the present-day town of **Forty Fort, PA**. As it happened, colonists in Pennsylvania had already begun to settle in the region. Fighting broke out between the two factions, ending with the Connecticut faction taking control. They weren't in control for long, however. When the Revolutionary War started, both the British and the Indians began fighting against the American colonists, and the settlers were driven out. At the close of the war, the Indians in turn were driven out by the Revolutionary Army, and the dispute between Connecticut and Pennsylvania was arbitrated by a special commission finding in favor of the latter.

Having great strategic importance during the Civil War, **Fort Morgan, AL**, (named in honor of Revolutionary War General Daniel Morgan) provided protection for the port city of Mobile. In 1864, Admiral David Farragut fought a protracted battle before taking the fort for the North. It was during this battle of Mobile Bay, when Farragut's flagship hit an underwater mine, that he uttered his famous command, "Damn the torpedoes! Full speed ahead!"

Fort Benton, MT, is named for Thomas H. Benton, who served as lawyer for John Jacob Astor's American Fur Company, which operated in the area. Fort Benton has since lent its name to a kind of clay called bentonite. Used in products like ceramics, soaps, insecticides, and paper manufacturing, this aluminum silicate material has the attribute of being able to absorb moisture, swelling when wet to several times its original size.

Fort Lee, NJ, named for Major General Charles Lee, was built in a vain effort to prevent the British from going up the Hudson River to West Point during the Revolutionary War. At one time in the early 1900s, Fort Lee served as the center of American silent film production. Prior to World War I, the town boasted seven studios and twenty-one film companies.

The sparsely populated rural area known as **Fort Lonesome, FL**, was, in fact, never a fort. Apparently the operative word in the name is "lonesome."

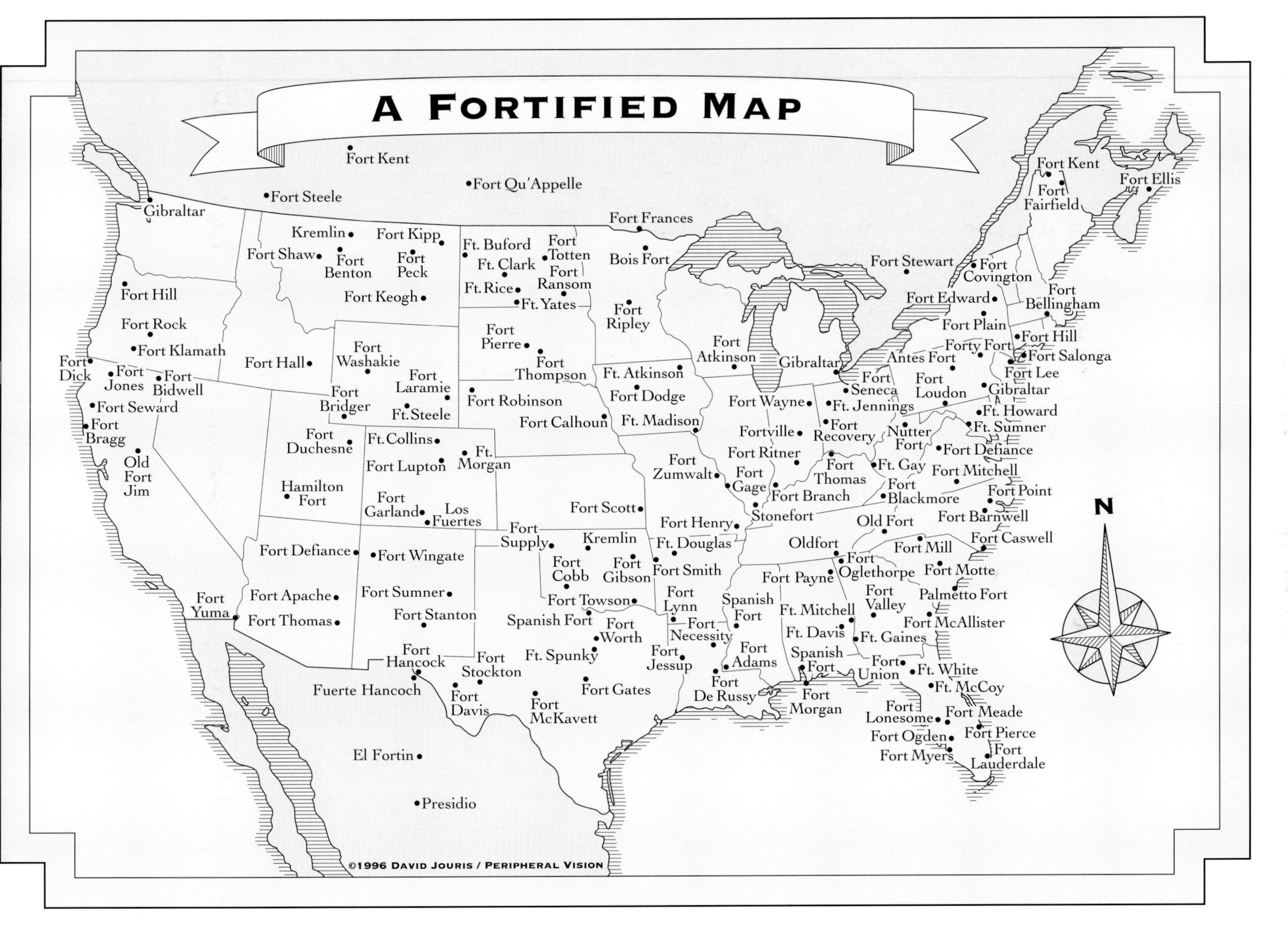

A FORTIFIED MAP
Fort Kent
Fort Qu'Appelle
Fort Steele
Gibraltar
Fort Frances
Kremlin
Fort Kipp
Fort Shaw
Fort Benton
Fort Peck
Ft. Buford
Fort Totten
Ft. Clark
Fort Ransom
Bois Fort
Ft. Rice
Ft. Yates
Fort Keogh
Fort Hill
Fort Rock
Fort Klamath
Fort Dick
Fort Jones
Fort Bidwell
Fort Hall
Fort Washakie
Fort Pierre
Fort Thompson
Fort Ripley
Fort Laramie
Fort Bridger
Ft. Steele
Fort Robinson
Fort Seward
Fort Bragg
Fort Duchesne
Ft. Collins
Ft. Morgan
Fort Lupton
Fort Calhoun
Ft. Atkinson
Fort Dodge
Ft. Madison
Fort Atkinson
Gibraltar
Old Fort Jim
Hamilton Fort
Fort Garland
Los Fuertes
Fort Scott
Fort Supply
Kremlin
Fort Defiance
Fort Wingate
Fort Cobb
Fort Gibson
Ft. Douglas
Fort Smith
Fort Henry
Fort Yuma
Fort Apache
Fort Thomas
Fort Sumner
Fort Stanton
Fort Towson
Spanish Fort
Fort Worth
Fort Lynn
Fort Necessity
Ft. Spunky
Fort Hancock
Fort Stockton
Fuerte Hancoch
Fort Davis
Fort McKavett
Fort Gates
Fort Jessup
Fort De Russy
Fort Adams
El Fortin
Presidio
Fort Zumwalt
Fort Gage
Fort Wayne
Fortville
Fort Ritner
Ft. Jennings
Fort Recovery
Fort Thomas
Fort Branch
Stonefort
Fort Seneca
Fort Stewart
Fort Covington
Fort Edward
Fort Plain
Fort Bellingham
Fort Hill
Forty Fort
Antes Fort
Fort Salonga
Fort Lee
Fort Loudon
Gibraltar
Ft. Howard
Ft. Sumner
Nutter Fort
Fort Defiance
Ft. Gay
Fort Mitchell
Fort Blackmore
Fort Point
Fort Barnwell
Old Fort
Fort Caswell
Fort Mill
Oldfort
Fort Oglethorpe
Fort Payne
Fort Motte
Fort Valley
Palmetto Fort
Spanish Fort
Ft. Mitchell
Fort McAllister
Ft. Davis
Ft. Gaines
Spanish Fort
Fort Union
Ft. White
Fort Morgan
Ft. McCoy
Fort Lonesome
Fort Meade
Fort Ogden
Fort Pierce
Fort Myers
Fort Lauderdale
Fort Kent
Fort Fairfield
Fort Ellis
N

From the sublime to the ridiculous is but a step.
—**Napoleon Bonaparte**

Those which are victorious.
—**Napoleon Bonaparte**, *on what troops he considered the best*

Austerlitz, NY, was named by President Martin Van Buren. Hearing that another town had recently been named Waterloo after the famous battle where Wellington defeated Napoleon, Van Buren, who hadn't forgotten France's assistance during the American Revolution, wanted to make sure there was a town named after one of Napoleon's great victories. Consequently, Van Buren saw to it that his own hometown took the name of Austerlitz, commemorating the French General's defeat of the Russian and Austrian armies at Austerlitz, Czechoslovakia.

The community of **Moscow, MN**, was named after a forest called Moscow Timber that became so-known because of a fire there in the mid 1800s, reminiscent of the fire in Moscow that burned as Napoleon retreated from the city. Similarly, the town of **Moscow, ME**, took its name when residents heard the news of Napoleon's retreat from Moscow.

It was a soldier who had been in charge of Napoleon's artillery at Waterloo, and who later emigrated to the United States, who named **Napoleonville, LA**. Louisiana, by the way, is the only one of the fifty states whose legal system is based on the French Napoleonic Code—or civil law—rather than the English system of common law. (Basically, civil law is based on legislative enactments, whereas common law is based upon the precident of previous judgments.)

Lodi, NJ, was named in 1825 by a dyer of French origin, Robert Rennie, in order to celebrate Napoleon's victory over the Austrians at the Bridge of Lodi, Italy, in 1796.

As a matter of related interest, it should be mentioned that it was Napoleon who was on the selling end of the Louisiana Purchase in 1803. The area gained by the United States constitutes what now includes some or all of the following states: Arkansas, Colorado, Iowa, Kansas, Louisiana, Minnesota, Missouri, Montana, Nebraska, North Dakota, Oklahoma, South Dakota, and Wyoming.

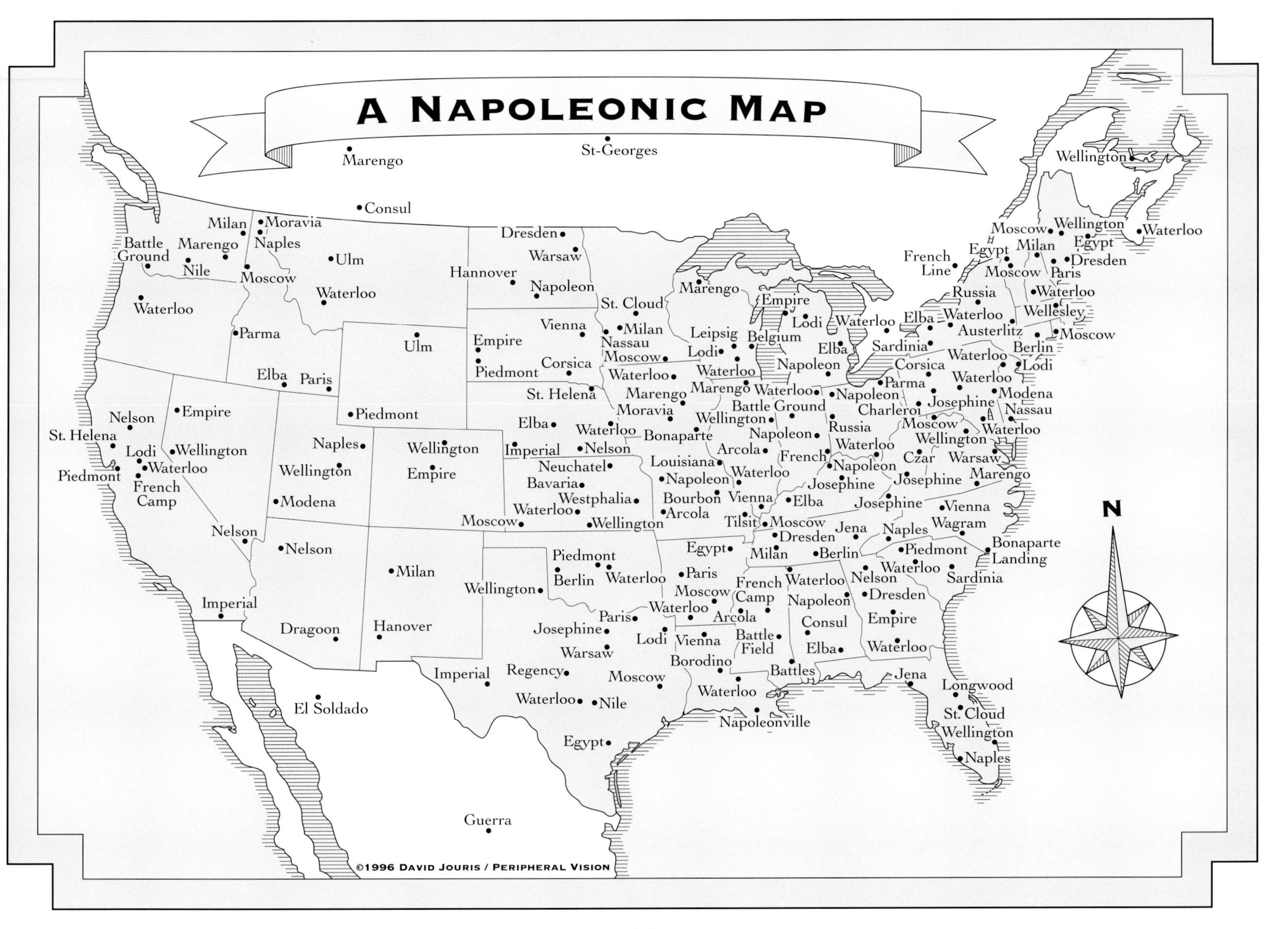

A NAPOLEONIC MAP
Marengo
St-Georges
Wellington
Consul
Milan
Moravia
Naples
Battle Ground
Marengo
Nile
Moscow
Ulm
Waterloo
Waterloo
Dresden
Warsaw
Hannover
Napoleon
Moscow
Wellington
Waterloo
Egypt
Milan
Egypt
Dresden
French Line
Moscow
Paris
Russia
Waterloo
Wellesley
Marengo
Empire
St. Cloud
Lodi
Waterloo
Elba
Waterloo
Austerlitz
Moscow
Parma
Ulm
Vienna
Milan
Nassau
Leipsig
Belgium
Sardinia
Berlin
Empire
Lodi
Elba
Waterloo
Lodi
Moscow
Napoleon
Corsica
Piedmont
Corsica
Waterloo
Waterloo
Elba
Paris
Marengo
Waterloo
Parma
Waterloo
Modena
St. Helena
Marengo
Napoleon
Josephine
Battle Ground
Charleroi
Nassau
Moravia
Wellington
Nelson
Empire
Piedmont
Elba
Moscow
Waterloo
St. Helena
Waterloo
Bonaparte
Napoleon
Russia
Wellington
Naples
Wellington
Imperial
Nelson
Arcola
Waterloo
Czar
Warsaw
Lodi
Wellington
Waterloo
Louisiana
French
Napoleon
Piedmont
Wellington
Neuchatel
Waterloo
Marengo
Empire
Napoleon
Josephine
Josephine
French Camp
Bavaria
Westphalia
Bourbon
Vienna
Elba
Josephine
Vienna
Modena
Waterloo
Arcola
Moscow
Wellington
Tilsit
Moscow
Jena
Naples
Wagram
Nelson
Dresden
Nelson
Egypt
Milan
Berlin
Piedmont
Bonaparte Landing
Piedmont
Berlin
Waterloo
Paris
Waterloo
Nelson
Sardinia
Milan
Wellington
Moscow
French Camp
Waterloo
Dresden
Imperial
Waterloo
Arcola
Napoleon
Paris
Empire
Dragoon
Hanover
Josephine
Lodi
Vienna
Battle Field
Consul
Warsaw
Elba
Waterloo
Borodino
Regency
Imperial
Moscow
Battles
Jena
Longwood
Waterloo
Waterloo
Nile
El Soldado
Napoleonville
St. Cloud
Wellington
Egypt
Naples
Guerra
N

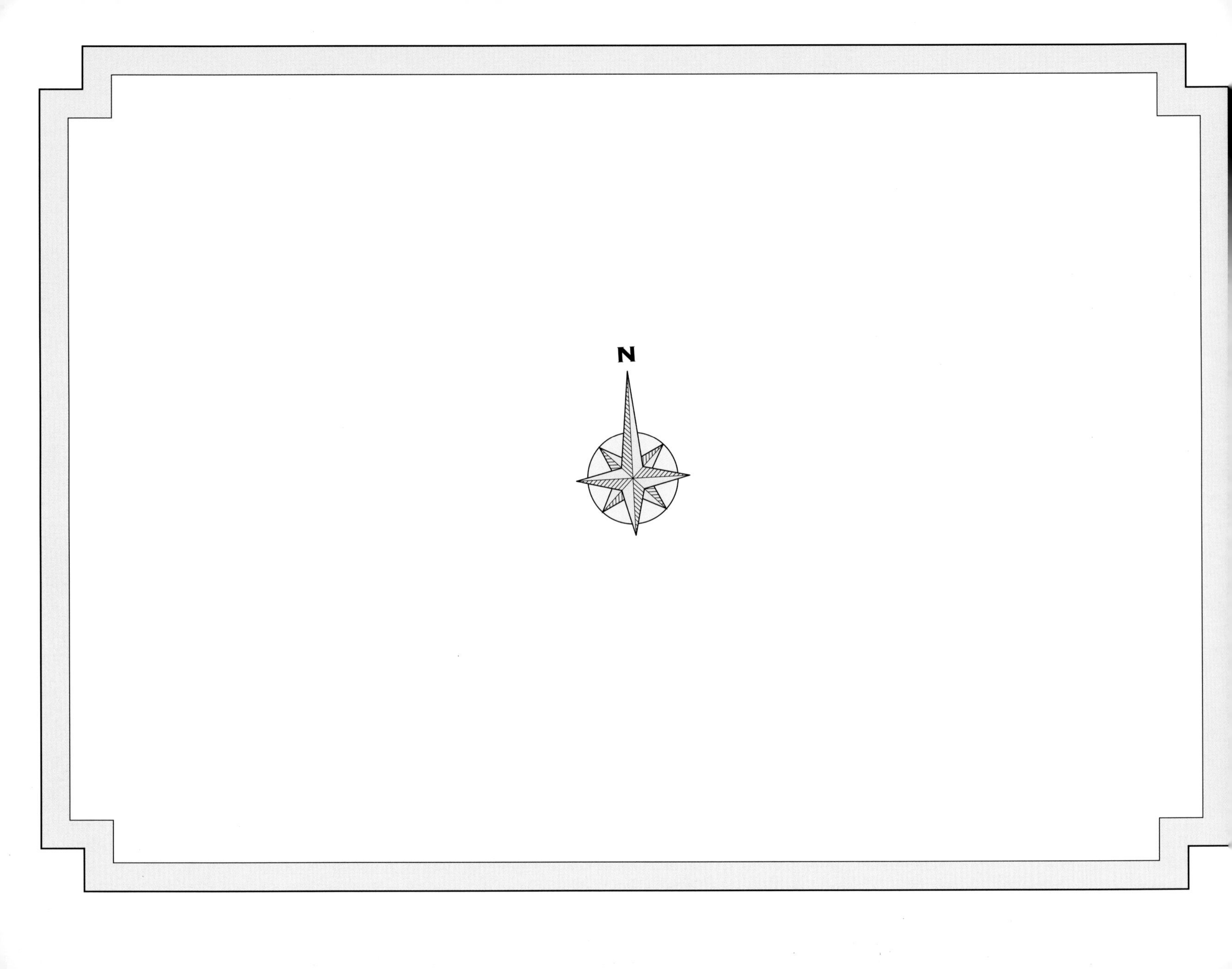
N

EVERYDAY MAPS

Maps that Transcend the Mundane

Some circumstantial evidence is very strong, as when you find a trout in the milk.

—HENRY DAVID THOREAU

The law, in its majesty, equally forbids the rich as well as the poor to sleep under bridges, to beg in the streets, and to steal bread.

—ANATOLE FRANCE

In colonial times, the location that eventually became **Lawyers, VA**, was midway along a road between New London County Courthouse and what is now Lynchburg. So many lawyers used this route that it came to be called Lawyers Road. Due to the distance between the main towns, traveling lawyers would spend the night at a tavern near the halfway point. When the railroad was laid through this area after the Civil War, a station was built next to the tavern and named Lawyers. The small community that grew up around it took the same name.

The region that now includes **Washington Court House, OH**, was once part of the Virginia Military Land District, a governmental area that provided land, in lieu of money, to people who fought in the Revolutionary War. The new settlers chose to name their community Washington; however, there was already at least one other town with that name in Ohio. The settlers used the common Virginia convention of distinguishing between like-named places by appending the words *Court House* to one of them.

Parole, MD, began as a camp set up by the federal government during the Civil War for soldiers released from Confederate prison camps as part of prisoner exchanges. Upon their return, the Union soldiers were processed here, given pay accrued during their absence, and mustered out. It speaks to people's tenacious memory that, although Camp Parole existed for only two years, the name has proven far more lasting.

In the mid 1800s it is said that many outlaws received a "suspended sentence" from the infamous hang tree in the town of Helena, MT. Lynchings like these were not uncommon at various times in the history of the United States. The term "to lynch," by the way, may derive from a Captain William Lynch, who was on a vigilance committee in Pittsylvania, VA, in the late 1700s. The methods of the vigilantees—involving condemnation without due process of law—often led to the hanging of the accused, as evidenced by the saying, "Give 'em a fair trial and then hang 'em."

The term "Philadephia lawyer" came about in 1743, in reference to the attorney for Peter Zenger, a New York publisher who was arrested and tried for criminal libel. (At the time, *truth* was no defense to this charge.) Zenger asked Andrew Hamilton, a distinguished lawyer from Philadelphia, to defend him. Hamilton obtained a *not guilty* verdict and thereby helped to lay the foundation for freedom of the press.

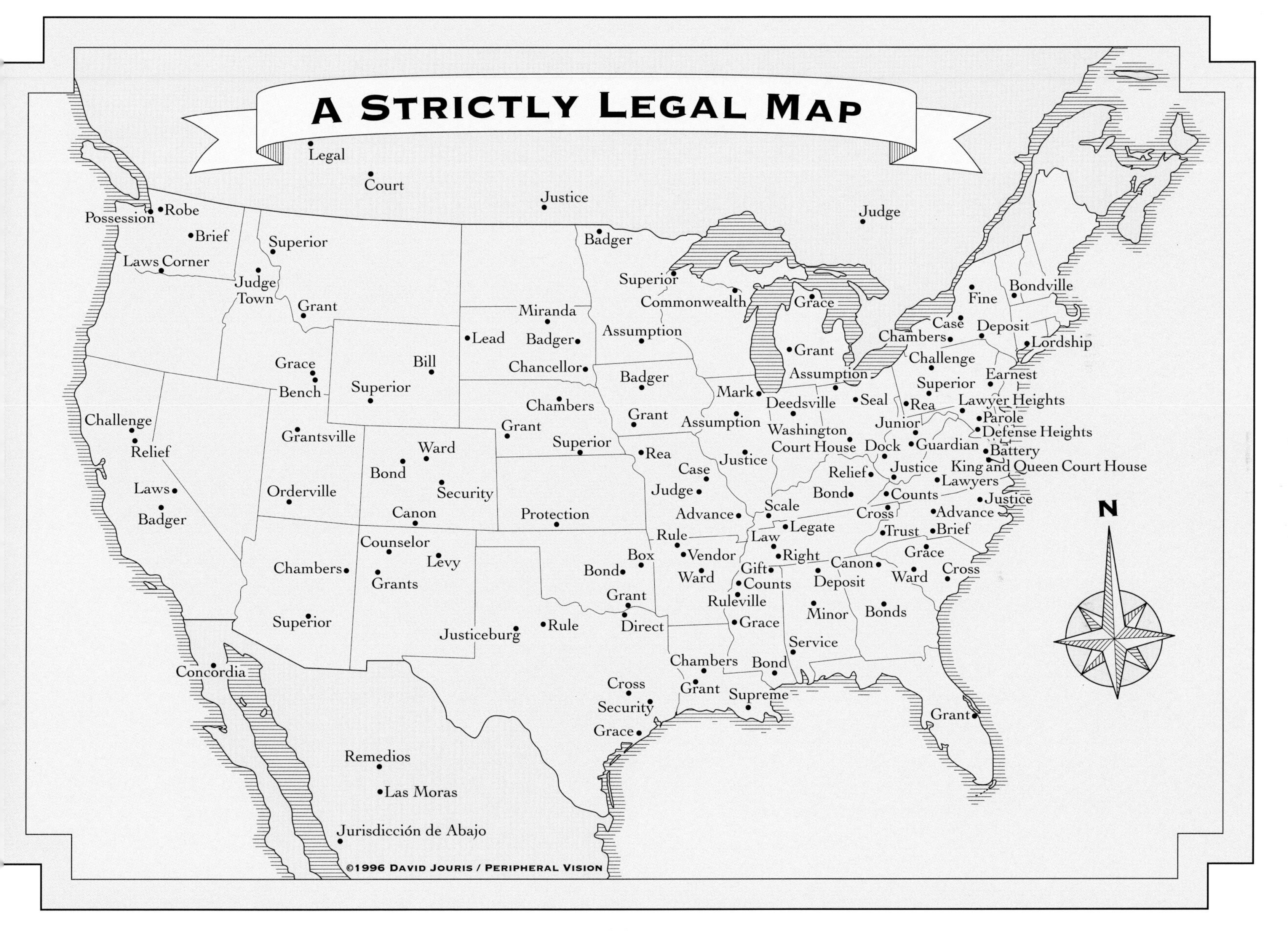
A STRICTLY LEGAL MAP
Legal
Court
Justice
Judge
Possession
Robe
Brief
Superior
Badger
Laws Corner
Judge Town
Superior
Commonwealth
Grace
Bondville
Fine
Grant
Miranda
Case
Deposit
Chambers
Lordship
Lead
Badger
Assumption
Grant
Challenge
Grace
Bill
Chancellor
Earnest
Bench
Superior
Badger
Assumption
Superior
Mark
Seal
Lawyer Heights
Deedsville
Rea
Chambers
Grant
Assumption
Junior
Parole
Challenge
Grant
Washington Court House
Defense Heights
Relief
Grantsville
Ward
Superior
Dock
Guardian
Battery
Rea
Justice
Bond
Case
Relief
Justice
King and Queen Court House
Laws
Orderville
Security
Judge
Lawyers
Badger
Bond
Counts
Justice
Canon
Protection
Advance
Scale
Cross
Advance
Legate
Trust
Brief
Counselor
Rule
Law
Levy
Box
Vendor
Right
Grace
Chambers
Bond
Canon
Cross
Grants
Ward
Gift
Ward
Counts
Deposit
Grant
Ruleville
Superior
Minor
Bonds
Rule
Direct
Grace
Justiceburg
Service
Concordia
Chambers
Bond
Cross
Grant
Security
Supreme
Grant
Grace
Remedios
Las Moras
Jurisdicción de Abajo
N
©1996 DAVID JOURIS / PERIPHERAL VISION

If all economists were laid end to end, they would not reach a conclusion.
—George Bernard Shaw

All my available funds are completely tied up in ready cash.
—W. C. Fields

In September, 1926, not far from **New Market, MN**, on old U. S. Highway 65, there appeared the first of the famous Burma Shave signs that would soon spread far and wide. The idea was dreamed up by Allan Odell, whose family had begun making the shaving cream. Allan and his brother Leonard took on the task of putting up the signs. (Recalling his job of digging holes for the signposts, Leonard claimed he learned about the family business "from three feet under the ground up.") The ads were set up in series of five or six signs in a row, spaced about 100 feet apart, with each sign bearing part of the jingle. Among the advertising rhymes:

- *Don't take a curve / At 60 per / We hate to lose / A customer. / Burma Shave.*
- *Past schoolhouses / Take it slow / Let the little / Shavers / Grow. / Burma Shave.*
- *A peach / Looks good / With lots of fuzz / But man's no peach / And never was. / Burma Shave.*

A modern, streamlined version of the Burma Shave concept—using a humorous billboard to relay a message—was erected in North Dakota a few years ago. One said, "Stay in North Dakota. Montana Closed This Week"; another sign in this mostly flat state proclaimed: "Welcome to North Dakota. Mountain Removal Project Completed." The campaign proved quite successful in putting North Dakota on the map—or in the minds of tourists, at any rate.

People in southwestern Georgia, when headed down Highway 97, are fully justified in saying that they are on the road to recovery. **Recovery, GA**, is a community of fewer than three dozen souls by Lake Seminole, near the Florida border.

The town of **Cash, TX**, was named by the president of the railroad. He originally wanted to call the place Money, after J.A. Money, a local shopkeeper. Too modest to accept this honor, Money suggested a synonymous name.

When the business leaders of **Tightwad, MO**, decided to open a bank, they went out on a limb and chose to make a blatant appeal to the miserly by naming it the Tightwad Bank. (One wonders if their loans are hard to come by.)

Speaking of banking, it's a little-known fact that the Bank of England was founded in Arkansas in 1898—in England, AR, to be exact. There actually was a fair amount of confusion between the little bank in Arkansas and the national bank in London, England, with mail for each occasionally being mistakenly delivered to the other. That confusion ended once the zip code system was implemented.

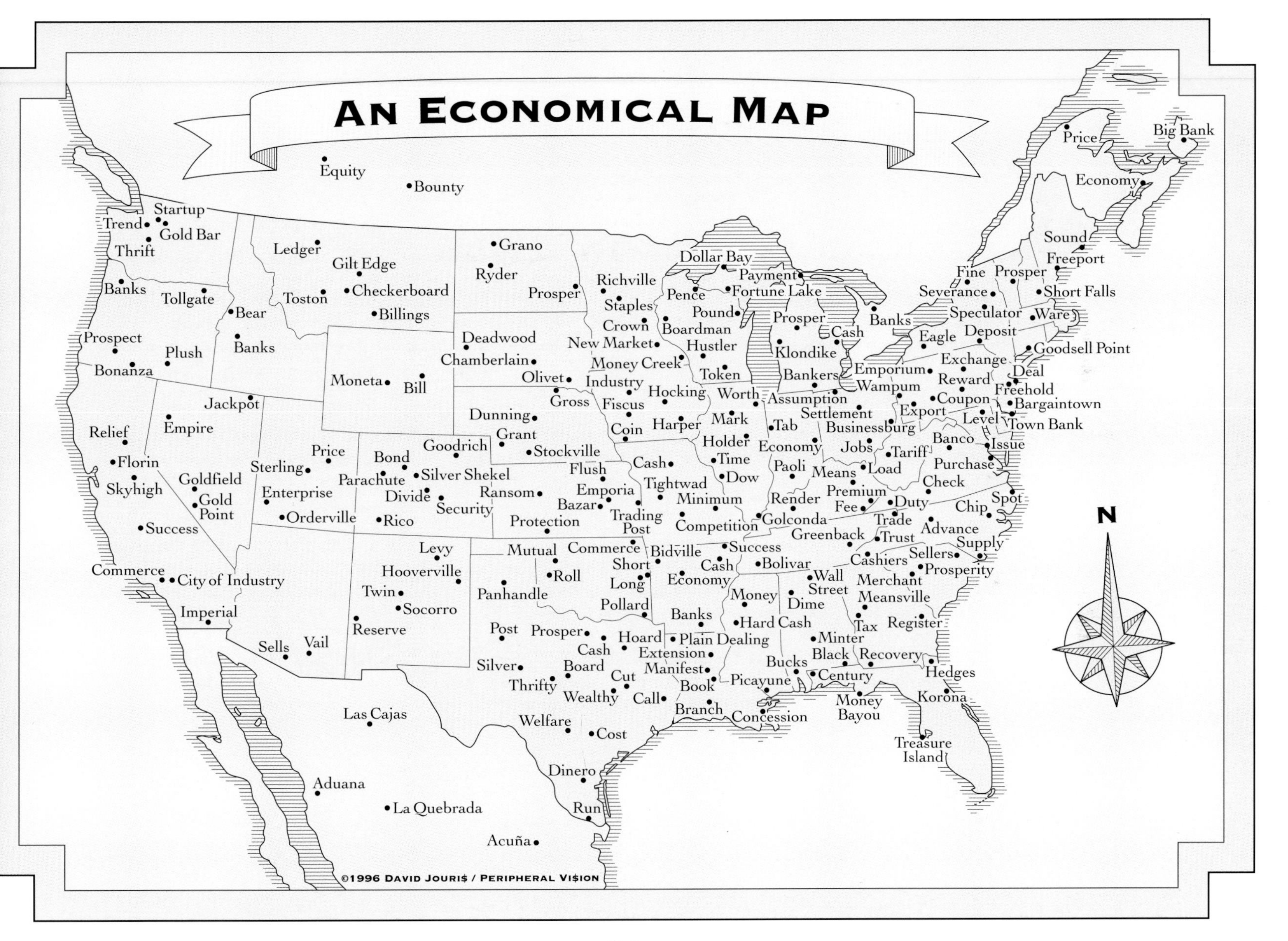
AN ECONOMICAL MAP
Equity
Bounty
Startup
Trend
Gold Bar
Thrift
Ledger
Grano
Gilt Edge
Ryder
Banks
Tollgate
Toston
Checkerboard
Billings
Bear
Prosper
Richville
Staples
Crown
New Market
Money Creek
Dollar Bay
Payment
Pence
Fortune Lake
Pound
Boardman
Hustler
Token
Prospect
Plush
Banks
Deadwood
Chamberlain
Olivet
Bonanza
Moneta
Bill
Industry
Gross
Fiscus
Coin
Hocking
Harper
Worth
Mark
Holder
Time
Dow
Jackpot
Empire
Relief
Florin
Skyhigh
Goldfield
Gold Point
Sterling
Enterprise
Orderville
Price
Bond
Parachute
Silver Shekel
Divide
Security
Rico
Goodrich
Dunning
Grant
Stockville
Flush
Ransom
Emporia
Bazar
Trading Post
Protection
Cash
Tightwad
Minimum
Competition
Success
Commerce
City of Industry
Imperial
Sells
Vail
Levy
Hooverville
Twin
Socorro
Reserve
Mutual
Roll
Panhandle
Commerce
Short
Long
Pollard
Bidville
Cash
Economy
Success
Bolivar
Post
Prosper
Cash
Hoard
Plain Dealing
Extension
Manifest
Silver
Thrifty
Board
Cut
Wealthy
Call
Book
Branch
Welfare
Cost
Dinero
Run
Las Cajas
Aduana
La Quebrada
Acuña
Money
Hard Cash
Banks
Dime
Wall Street
Picayune
Concession
Bucks
Century
Minter
Black
Money Bayou
Price
Big Bank
Economy
Sound
Freeport
Fine
Prosper
Short Falls
Severance
Speculator
Ware
Banks
Prosper
Cash
Klondike
Bankers
Eagle
Deposit
Goodsell Point
Exchange
Emporium
Wampum
Reward
Deal
Freehold
Coupon
Bargaintown
Assumption
Settlement
Export
Level
Town Bank
Tab
Businessburg
Economy
Banco
Issue
Jobs
Tariff
Purchase
Paoli
Means
Load
Check
Render
Premium
Fee
Duty
Chip
Spot
Golconda
Trade
Advance
Greenback
Trust
Supply
Cashiers
Sellers
Prosperity
Merchant
Meansville
Tax
Register
Recovery
Hedges
Korona
Treasure Island
N
©1996 DAVID JOURI$ / PERIPHERAL VI$ION

The race is not always to the swift, nor the battle to the strong—but that's the way to bet.
—DAMON RUNYON

I hope I break even this week. I need the money.
—ANONYMOUS GAMBLER

The town of **Deadwood, SD**, got its name because the first miners to arrive here in the 1870s found the area strewn with dead trees, the result of lightning-ignited fires. Some of the people coming to this mining community in its early years found gold—and some found lead. Wild Bill Hickok had only been in town a few weeks when he was shot and killed while playing cards. Legend has it that Hickok was holding a pair of aces and a pair of eights when he died—subsequently, aces-and-eights have been referred to as a "deadman's hand." By the way, *deadwood* is a term gamblers use to signify useless cards.

Since gambling has long been legal in Nevada, it is not hard to guess how **Jackpot, NV**, got its name. Although a "jackpot" is usually thought of as the result of hitting the winning combination on a slot machine, the word comes from a type of draw poker in which one must have a pair of jacks or better to open the betting. It sometimes takes a few rounds before anyone can bet, but with each hand the players must ante; as a result, the pot can increase significantly before the actual betting begins.

Luck, WI, was founded as a stopping place for settlers traveling between Cumberland, WI, and Taylors Falls, MN, on the St. Croix River, where their supplies were delivered by boat. The journey took at least two days, and travelers felt they were in "luck" if they got to this point by the end of the first day. An apocryphal story of how the town got its name holds that the town's founder declared, "I propose to be in luck the rest of my life."

It is unlikely that the name **Buck, PA**, originated with gambling, but let's overlook that for the nonce. In gambling parlance, the word *buck* is a shortening of *buckhorn knife*, an object formerly used in poker to designate the next player to deal. Hence the expression "to pass the buck," meaning to pass responsibility for something on to someone else.

A GAMBLING MAP
Casino
Ideal
Port Gamble
Index
Royal
Diamond
Sodaville
Post
Bridge
Diamond
Sixes
Keno
Fields
Bluff Creek
Banks
King Hill
Bridge
Jackpot
Hedgesville
Racetrack
Trotters
Napoleon
Casino
Deadwood
Lead
Wall
Winner
Diamondville
Diamond
Saratoga
Centennial
Royal
King Lake
Hazard
Last Chance
Bridgeland
Poker Flat
Flush
Bluff
Bluff City
Straight
Roll
Bell
Show Low
House
Roll
Black
Spade
New Deal
Post
Draw
Queen
El Paso
Poolville
Maverick
Wall
Cash
Point
Bluff
Box
Bunch
Welch
Pack
Diamond
Edge
Cut
Ace
Call
Bridge City
Nursery
Run
La Fortuna
Suerte
La Paz
©1996 DAVID JOURIS / PERIPHERAL VISION
Luck
Ubet
Hustler
Kings Park
Rake
Royal
High
Mark
Cash
Case
Blackjack
Diamond
Heartville
Block
Kokomo
Black
Diamond
Black
Game
Heart
Pontoon
Royal
Gin City
Banks
Lucky
Book
Bankers
Diamond
Cardsville
Longshot
Hand
Kings
Rondo
Honor
Palms
Commerce
Bankers
Roll
Diamond Trail
Diamond
Spades
Cincinnati
Bidwell
Stay
Chance
Dice
Odd
Barrier
Winner
Lucky
Luck
Calls
Pool
Cash
Gamble
Bridgeville
Jack
Chance
Black
Bluff Springs
Bell
Cutting
Roulette
Dice
Gap
Deal
Buck
Deal
Joker
Banco
Spread
Sabot
Check
Ante
Faro
King
Chip
Queen
Shuffletown
Lucknow
Broadway
Centennial
Blackjack
Hedges
Royal
Queens Cove
Kings Creek
Mechanicsville
Chance
Chance
Deck
Index
Calcutta
Banksville
Mechanicsville
Derby
Levant
Gagné
N

Mathematics is the science in which one never knows what one is talking about, nor whether what one is saying is true.
—**BERTRAND RUSSELL**

I see the shapes I remember from maps.
—**DAVID BYRNE**, "The Big Country"

Paradox, CO, derives its name from Paradox Valley, in which it sits. Paradox Valley is so called because a river cuts through its sheer red cliff walls at right angles, creating a very striking sight. Early settlers had a tough time getting into the valley because of these steep cliffs, and had to unload their belongings, disassemble their wagons, and lower everything down piece by piece using ropes. It's hard to say whether a place like this discourages or encourages "drop-in" visitors.

Originally, the town of **Circleville, OH**, was set in a location with two large ancient earthworks—one square-shaped, the other circular with a moat around it. The town was built inside the circle, with an octagon-shaped courthouse in the center and a pattern of concentric circular streets radiating outward. As time passed, the citizens began to realize two big problems with their circular town. To begin with, the water sitting in the moat was creating health problems, and second, the pie-shaped lots were awkward to use efficiently. Eventually, the moat was eliminated and—in spite of skeptics who think it impossible for a town to convince its citizens to accept the reconfiguring of their property—the lots were reshaped, section by section, along more conventional lines as the town squared the circle. (Unfortunately for pessimistic hipsters everywhere, the town's name didn't follow suit and get changed to Squaresville.)

Tangent, OR, derives its name from its location along a twenty-mile stretch of straight train track—a "tangent" in railroad lingo. Also railroad-related is the origin of the name **Diagonal, IA**. The name refers to a new track laid to run diagonally to an existing railroad line.

The town of **Oblong, IL**, was previously named Henpeck to honor a resident named Henry Peck, but the name's connotation began to make some residents uncomfortable. It is said that the new name of Oblong was chosen because that was the basic geometric shape of the town. The residents aren't completely free of unintended meanings cropping up; newspapers in the area still carry an occasional story with a headline like "Normal Man Marries Oblong Woman"—with reference to Normal, IL, in this case.

A Mathematical Map

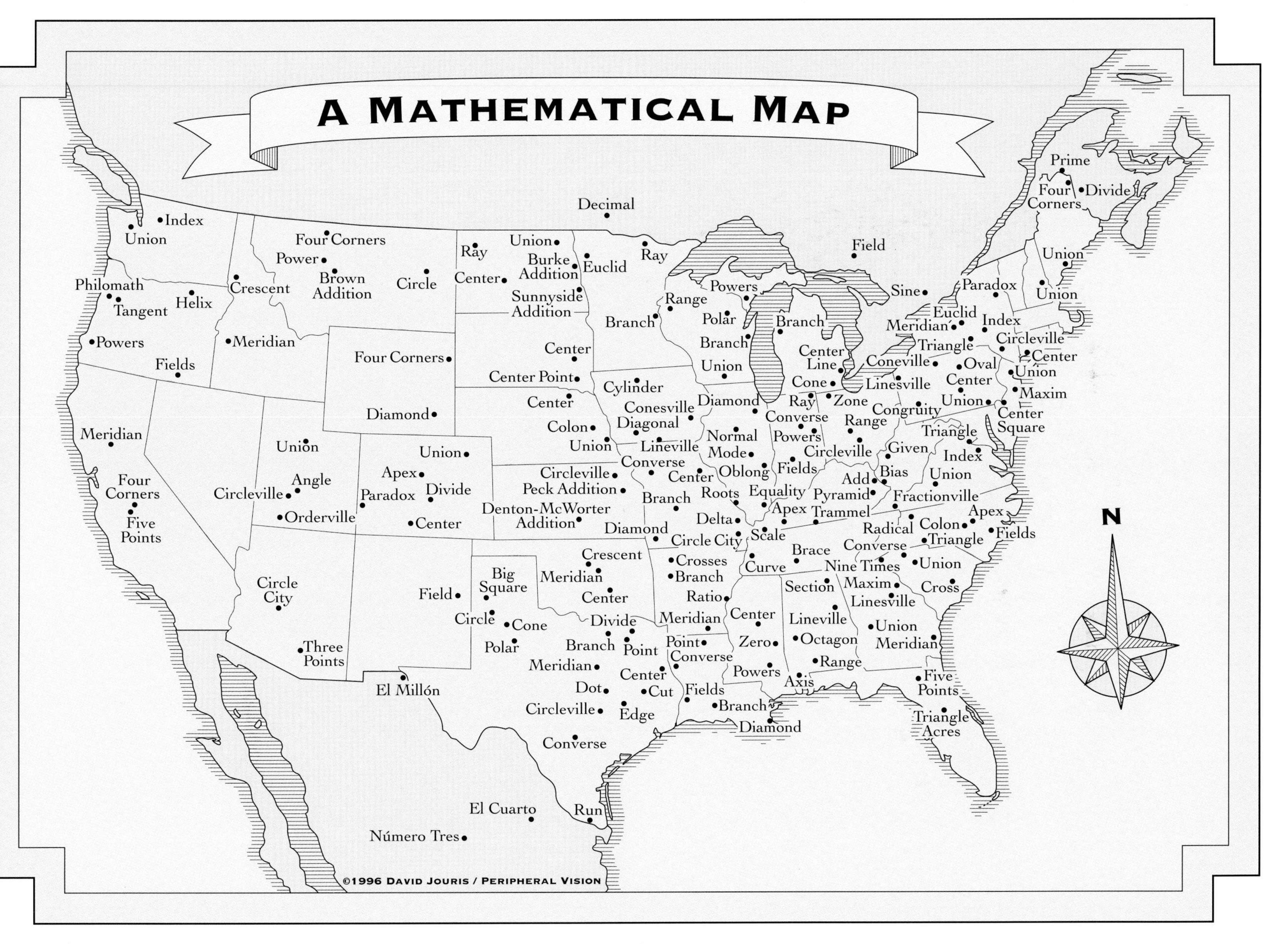

Everything in life is somewhere else, and you get there in a car.
—E. B. White

Our national flower is the concrete cloverleaf.
—Lewis Mumford

Conestoga, PA, is located in the valley where the like-named covered wagons were designed and built. One aspect of the design perched the driver on a board extending out on the front left side of the wagon. Interestingly, this may be the origin of our custom of having the steering wheel set on the left side of our vehicles. Teamsters may have also helped originate a familiar phrase, according to some authorities: it was standard practice for a Conestoga driver to attach brass bells to the harness of his team of pulling horses, and an unfortunate driver who got stuck in the mud would give up the horses' bells to the teamster who helped pull the wagon out. Thus, if a wagon arrived at its destination "with bells on," it signified a trip made without incident. The town also became famous for its cigars, originally called the *Conestoga cigar*, but eventually shortened to *stogie*.

One hears two stories of how **Auto, WV**, got its name. The first goes that automobiles were tested here because the area had the only flat two-mile stretch of road in the world. As it turns out, however, there is no truth to this; only a very narrow, windy, hilly road runs through the community. The second story, with at least some foundation in fact, is that the post- master wanted to name the town after his dog, Otto. Unfortunately, there was already a place in West Virginia named Otto, so the homophone was used.

The community of **Double Tollgate, VA**, is located where the crossroads of two turnpikes existed from the mid 1800s until the early 1900s. Because this place was at the intersection, two different tolls could be collected, depending upon which route was being used. The word *turnpike* comes from the turnstiles used at the entrances to private roads in America. A turnstile consisted of a pole, or pike, that turned on an axle to admit a traveler's wagon. The term *shunpike* comes from the alternate trails created to avoid, or shun, the tollhouses.

Steamboat, NV, is named for the hot mineral springs nearby. Early settlers said that on some days there were sixty or seventy columns of steam rising dozens of feet into the air, and the constant rumbling noise created by the water was similar to that of a steamboat.

Exactly how **Detour, MD**, came by its name is uncertain. What is known is that the town used to be named Double Pipe Creek Village. The railroad felt that name was too long and asked for a shorter name. It would be fair to assume that the present name came as a result of trying to get around the problems created by the former name.

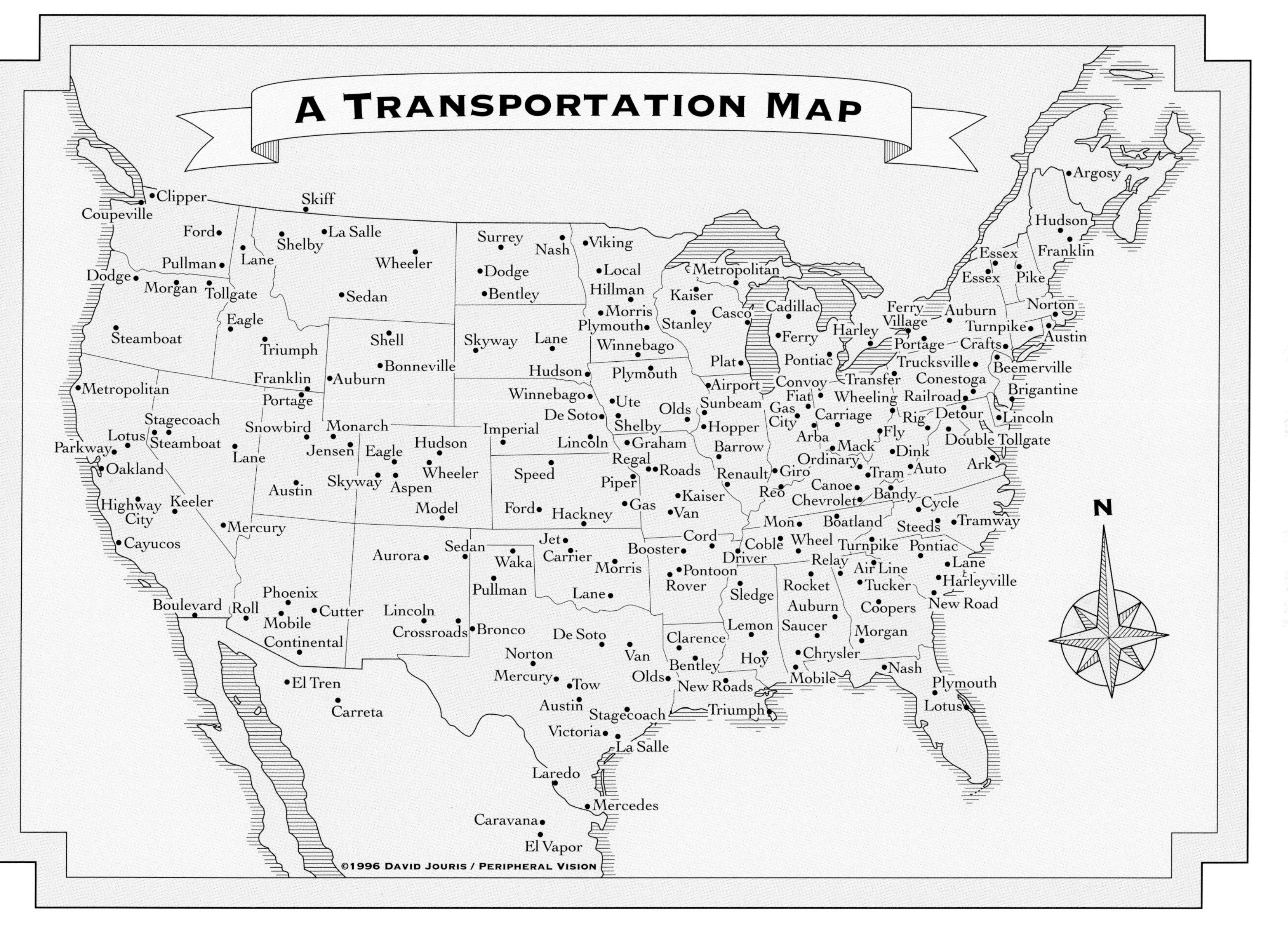
A TRANSPORTATION MAP
Argosy
Clipper
Skiff
Coupeville
Ford
La Salle
Shelby
Lane
Surrey
Nash
Viking
Hudson
Franklin
Wheeler
Pullman
Dodge
Local
Essex
Essex
Pike
Dodge
Morgan
Tollgate
Sedan
Bentley
Hillman
Metropolitan
Kaiser
Cadillac
Norton
Morris
Casco
Ferry Village
Auburn
Eagle
Steamboat
Triumph
Shell
Skyway
Lane
Plymouth
Stanley
Ferry
Harley
Turnpike
Austin
Portage
Crafts
Winnebago
Pontiac
Trucksville
Beemerville
Bonneville
Hudson
Plymouth
Plat
Franklin
Auburn
Convoy
Transfer
Conestoga
Metropolitan
Airport
Brigantine
Portage
Winnebago
Ute
Sunbeam
Fiat
Wheeling
Railroad
Stagecoach
Olds
Gas City
Carriage
Rig
Detour
Lincoln
De Soto
Snowbird
Monarch
Imperial
Shelby
Hopper
Arba
Fly
Lotus
Steamboat
Double Tollgate
Parkway
Jensen
Eagle
Hudson
Lincoln
Graham
Barrow
Mack
Dink
Lane
Regal
Ordinary
Ark
Oakland
Wheeler
Speed
Roads
Renault
Giro
Tram
Auto
Skyway
Aspen
Piper
Austin
Canoe
Keeler
Kaiser
Reo
Bandy
Highway City
Chevrolet
Cycle
Model
Ford
Gas
Hackney
Van
Mercury
Mon
Boatland
Steeds
Tramway
Cord
Jet
Wheel
Cayucos
Sedan
Coble
Turnpike
Pontiac
Aurora
Waka
Carrier
Booster
Driver
Relay
Lane
Morris
Air Line
Pontoon
Tucker
Harleyville
Rover
Rocket
Pullman
Phoenix
Sledge
Lane
Boulevard
Roll
Cutter
Auburn
Coopers
New Road
Lincoln
Mobile
Saucer
Lemon
Crossroads
Bronco
De Soto
Morgan
Continental
Clarence
Norton
Van
Chrysler
Hoy
Bentley
Nash
Mercury
Tow
Olds
Mobile
Plymouth
El Tren
New Roads
Austin
Lotus
Carreta
Stagecoach
Triumph
Victoria
La Salle
Laredo
Mercedes
Caravana
El Vapor
N
©1996 DAVID JOURIS / PERIPHERAL VISION

What are the natural features which make a township handsome? A river, with its waterfalls and meadows, a lake, a hill, a cliff or individual rocks, a forest, and ancient trees standing singly. Such things are beautiful....
—HENRY DAVID THOREAU

For purple mountain majesties above the fruited plain! America! America!
—KATHARINE LEE BATES

In May of 1869, at **Promontory, UT**, railroad tycoon Leland Stanford was given the honor of marking the completion of America's first transcontinental railroad by using a silver-headed maul to pound a golden spike into the final railroad tie. Stanford managed to completely miss the spike, but eventually a group effort got the job done. The name of the town comes from the Promontory mountain range, where the town is located. The range itself is so-called because of a long, rocky section that juts into the northern end of the Great Salt Lake.

Beginning more than 2,000 years ago, several different mound-building Native American cultures arose in North America, including the Adena, Hopewell, and Mississippian people. The Indians built both temple and burial mounds, a number of which are still visible along rivers like the Mississippi and the Ohio. Among the large earthworks that remain is the Great Serpent Mound in southwestern Ohio. This undulating figure is made of earth five feet high, twenty feet wide, and almost a quarter of a mile long. The temple mounds at **Moundville, AL**, cover some 300 acres and are thought to have been the center of a Mississippian culture with as many as 10,000 people. The Moundville site consists of nineteen mounds, including one that is over fifty feet high. At **Moundsville, WV**, is a mound that's almost seventy feet high; its construction involved moving 57,000 tons of soil. **Mound City, MO**, is named for the presence of several ancient funeral mounds. The largest Indian earthwork in North America is here: Mon's Mound covers fourteen acres and stands 100 feet high. Worth mentioning too is Cahokia Mounds State Historic Site near Collinsville, IL, which has some sixty ceremonial and burial mounds—all that remain of what was once the largest Native American city north of Mexico.

Although there are some active volcanoes on the west coast, **Volcano, CA**, takes its name from what was mistakenly thought to have been a volcano but in fact wasn't. Still, to the untrained eye, the natural rock formations in the area *do* suggest once-molten rock.

In the 1890s, the first white settlers arrived in the area around Mt. Baker, in the Pacific Northwest. As a community formed, they named it **Glacier, WA**, because it is sited on Glacier Creek, which is fed by (and named for) the large formation of ice on the mountain.

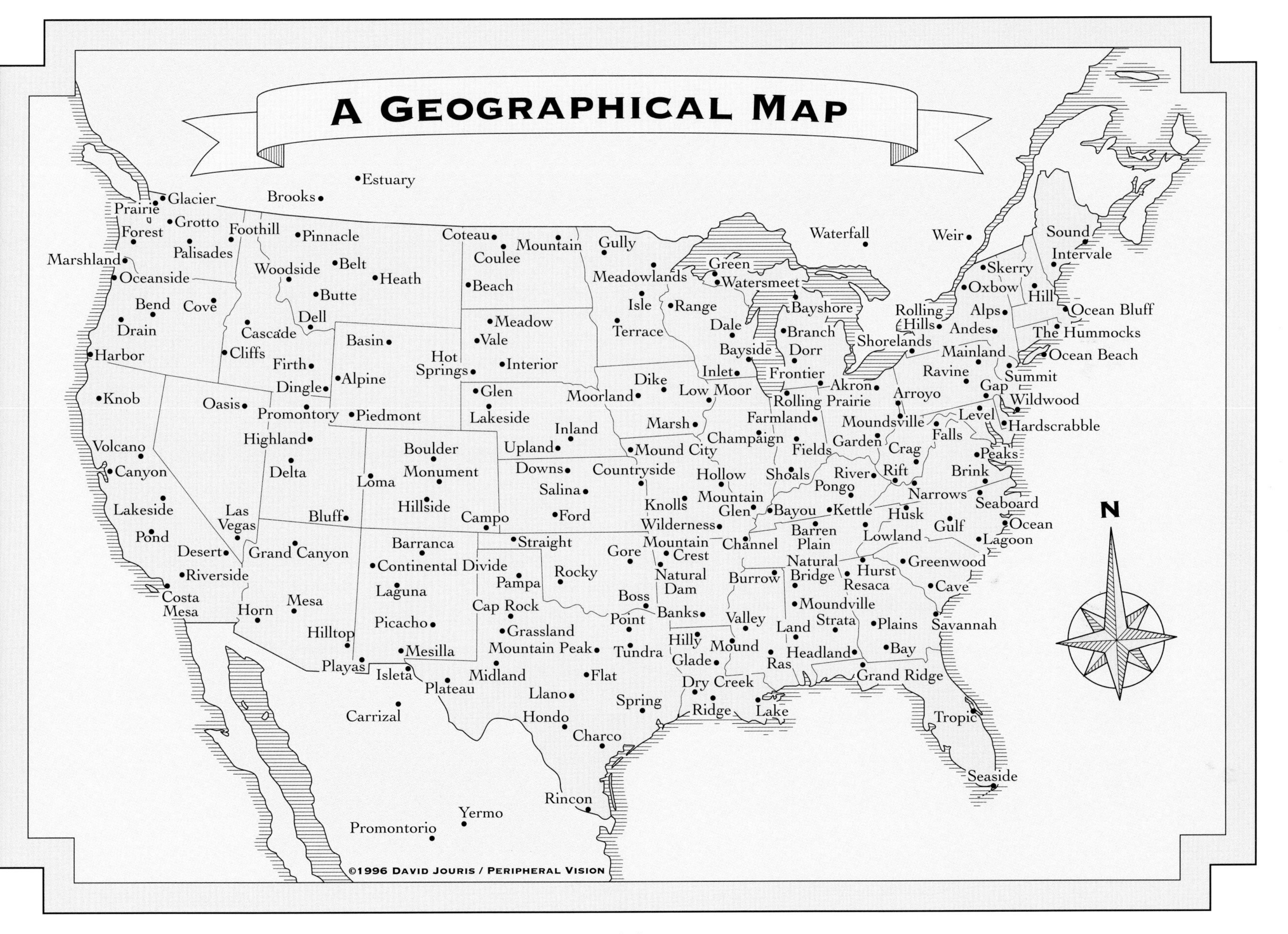
A GEOGRAPHICAL MAP
Estuary
Brooks
Glacier
Prairie
Grotto
Forest
Foothill
Pinnacle
Palisades
Marshland
Oceanside
Woodside
Belt
Heath
Butte
Bend
Cove
Drain
Dell
Cascade
Basin
Harbor
Cliffs
Firth
Alpine
Dingle
Knob
Oasis
Promontory
Piedmont
Highland
Volcano
Canyon
Delta
Lakeside
Las Vegas
Pond
Desert
Grand Canyon
Riverside
Costa Mesa
Horn
Mesa
Hilltop
Playas
Bluff
Loma
Boulder
Monument
Hillside
Barranca
Continental Divide
Laguna
Picacho
Mesilla
Isleta
Plateau
Carrizal
Promontorio
Yermo
Coteau
Coulee
Mountain
Beach
Meadow
Vale
Hot Springs
Interior
Glen
Lakeside
Campo
Straight
Pampa
Cap Rock
Grassland
Mountain Peak
Midland
Upland
Downs
Salina
Ford
Rocky
Inland
Moorland
Gully
Meadowlands
Isle
Range
Terrace
Dike
Low Moor
Marsh
Mound City
Countryside
Knolls
Wilderness
Mountain
Crest
Gore
Natural Dam
Boss
Point
Banks
Tundra
Flat
Llano
Hondo
Charco
Spring
Rincon
Hilly
Glade
Dry Creek
Ridge
Lake
Green
Watersmeet
Dale
Bayside
Inlet
Waterfall
Bayshore
Branch
Dorr
Frontier
Akron
Rolling Prairie
Farmland
Champaign
Fields
Hollow
Shoals
Mountain
Glen
Bayou
Channel
Barren Plain
Natural Bridge
Burrow
Moundville
Valley
Land
Strata
Mound
Headland
Ras
Pongo
River
Kettle
Garden
Moundsville
Crag
Rift
Narrows
Husk
Lowland
Hurst
Resaca
Greenwood
Cave
Plains
Bay
Savannah
Grand Ridge
Tropic
Seaside
Shorelands
Rolling Hills
Arroyo
Falls
Weir
Skerry
Oxbow
Alps
Andes
Mainland
Ravine
Gap
Level
Peaks
Brink
Seaboard
Gulf
Ocean
Lagoon
Sound
Intervale
Hill
Ocean Bluff
The Hummocks
Ocean Beach
Summit
Wildwood
Hardscrabble
N
©1996 DAVID JOURIS / PERIPHERAL VISION

As an instrument of planetary home repair, it is hard to imagine anything as safe as a tree.
—JONATHAN WEINER

The tree casts its shade upon all, even upon the woodcutter.
—SANSKRIT PROVERB

Lemon Grove, CA, has a name that, one would assume, came from the presence of lemon groves there. Actually, it was named before any lemon trees were planted. Although the landowner thought the climate would be suitable for lemons, he was more interested in luring people to the new town site and he wanted a name with appeal. In the late nineteenth century, a trend developed in southern California to lure people out from the east with the promise of an easy life: one didn't really have to work, just plant trees and watch the fruit grow. A number of lemon groves were eventually planted in Lemon Grove, although, like so much of the land in southern California, those trees have now been cut down to make room for housing. The only visible sign of the citrus fruit, besides the town name, is a ten-foot replica of a lemon that sits in the middle of town. What Lemon Grove does have, it claims without undue modesty, is the "best climate on earth."

Borrowing from the botanical name for the beech tree is **Fagus, MO**. This term was chosen in order to avoid the likelihood of duplication by another place. The town was previously called Slapout—a name that wouldn't seem to have been in much danger of duplication, either.

Marked Tree, AR, is named for a large oak tree along the St. Francis River. The tree was marked in order to signify the best place to pull into shore for traffic heading upriver. From here one could haul a canoe or dugout across a quarter mile of land to connect with a tributary called the Little River. Otherwise, a traveler would have about a dozen winding miles of paddling or poling against the river's current.

Along a slough northeast of San Francisco is the last remaining Chinese village in North America—**Walnut Grove, CA**. (The area is similar to the Pearl River Delta in China, where the first immigrants came from.) The Chinese helped to change the California Delta area from a region of swamps into the agricultural success story it is today. They built the levees, floodgates, and drainage ditches, and then worked on the local farms.

Joshua Tree, CA, is named for the desert tree that is plentiful in the area. The tree got its name from Mormon pioneers who, after what may have been a bit too much time in the desert sun, imagined that this evergreen plant with its unusual branches bore a resemblance to Joshua pointing the way to the Promised Land.

A TREE-COVERED MAP
Forestburg
Forestville
Treesbank
Chico
Fir Tree
Manzanita
Sumach
Orchards
Witch Hazel
Kamela
Lime
Nyssa
Tiller
Evergreen
Lonepine
Syringa
Yellow Pine
Alder
Laurel
Olive
Poplar
Pembina
Silva
Mott
Woods
Linden Grove
Tamarack
Birch
Ironwood
Hardwood
Flambeau
Arbor Vitae
Spruce
Cedar
Copas
Sugar Bush
Branch
Hemlock
Dilly
Red Elm
Whitewood
Box Elder
Hazel
Lone Tree
Doon
Salix
Linn Grove
Linden
Pepper Tree
Paw Paw
Castana
Cherry
Ross
Plum Tree
Beech
Pepperwood
Willows
Walnut Grove
Lotus
Buckeye
Redwood City
Holt
Sugar Pine
Aromas
Alamo
Acacia Acres
Sequoia Crest
Juniper
Cottonwood
Woodland
Wildwood
Big Piney
Pine Bluffs
Silver Spruce
Conifer
Aspen
Black Forest
Orchard
Wahoo
Oak
Burr Oak
Linn
Sylvan Grove
Holly
Palmyra
Chestnut
Windfall
Quercus Grove
Black Walnut
Roots
Viburnum
Mulberry
Birch Tree
Fagus
Hurst
Pyrus
Hackberry
Pomona
Joshua Tree
Thousand Palms
Lemon Grove
Pine
Nogales
Capulin
Mora
Amarillo
Maple
Pinon
Tornillo
Notrees
Vera
Blackgum
Red Oak
Apple
Yuba
Annona
Mesquite
Rosewood
Waterwood
Dogwood
Plum
Pollard
Marked Tree
Boles
Durian
Magnolia
Trees
Toro
Palmetto
Bel
Ama
Pecan Grove
Sugar Tree
Mimosa
White Pine
Tupelo
Shaw
Sabino
Forest
Leaf
Spruce Pine
Lightwood
Fig Tree
Catalpa
Blackwood
Cypress
Yates
Sandalwood
Live Oak
Woodland Grove
Orange
Woodsville
Redwood
Bayberry
Clove
Mapleville
Linden
Almond
Yulan
Birch Groves
Forest
Buttonwood
Branchville
Cork
Castanea
Elm
Locust
Candlewood
Redhaw
Cherry Tree
Pavia
Boxwood
Crooked Tree
Lignum
Quince Orchard
Cedron
Coco
Gimlet
Gum Tree
Pear
Ebony
Sassafras
Bundy
Roundtree
Hickory
Balsam
Ash
Filbert
White Oak
Calabash
Wampee
Persimmon
Elder
Sycamore
Silver Pines
Odum
Satsuma
Tangerine
Citronelle
Raintree
Poinciana
Mango
Palm Beach
El Durazano
Zapote
Los Pinos
Encinal
N
©1996 DAVID JOURIS / PERIPHERAL VISION

A good farmer is nothing more or less than
a handy man with a sense of humus.
—E. B. WHITE

America is ninety percent corn.
—ANDREW ERISH

Although it was probably named for the village of Farmington in Gloucestershire, England, the town of **Farmington, CT**, was itself primarily concerned with agriculture for much of the time since it was founded in 1640. Alas, in spite of Connecticut's nickname as "The Land of Steady Habits," there is not much farming in Farmington these days.

Farmington, ME, was named in the late 1700s by a settler who felt it was "a good farming region." Farmington is now a college town, so it is fair to surmise that these days there is more raising cain than raising corn. Coincidently, the town claims to be the Earmuff Capital of the World. Hometown boy Chester Greenwood invented the earmuff in 1873, at the age of fifteen. Greenwood went on to invent myriad other practical items—including a cotton picker, washing machine, folding bed, airplane shock absorber, and lawn rake—thus becoming one of the most prolific of American inventors, holding over 100 patents.

The town of **Ceres, CA**, was named in 1874 for the Roman goddess of grain by the daughter of one of the first settlers. Although the principal crops in the area around the town were originally wheat and barley, these days there is actually more emphasis on walnuts, almonds, and dairy products.

Also displaying a Roman flavor is **Agricola, MS**, employing the Latin word for "farmer." Appropriately enough, the town is located in the middle of a farming region. **Farmer, SD**, was named by an early settler because the area "seemed destined to become a farmers' paradise." And, although one might suspect that **Yeoman, IN**, was named to honor the small farmer who cultivates his own land, it was actually named for a local railroad official—Colonel Yeoman.

Cornfields, AZ, situated on the Navajo Reservation, is named for the Native Americans' cornfields. Although white corn is still prevalent there, the wheat that lent its name to nearby **Wheatfields, AZ**, has been mostly supplanted by alfalfa.

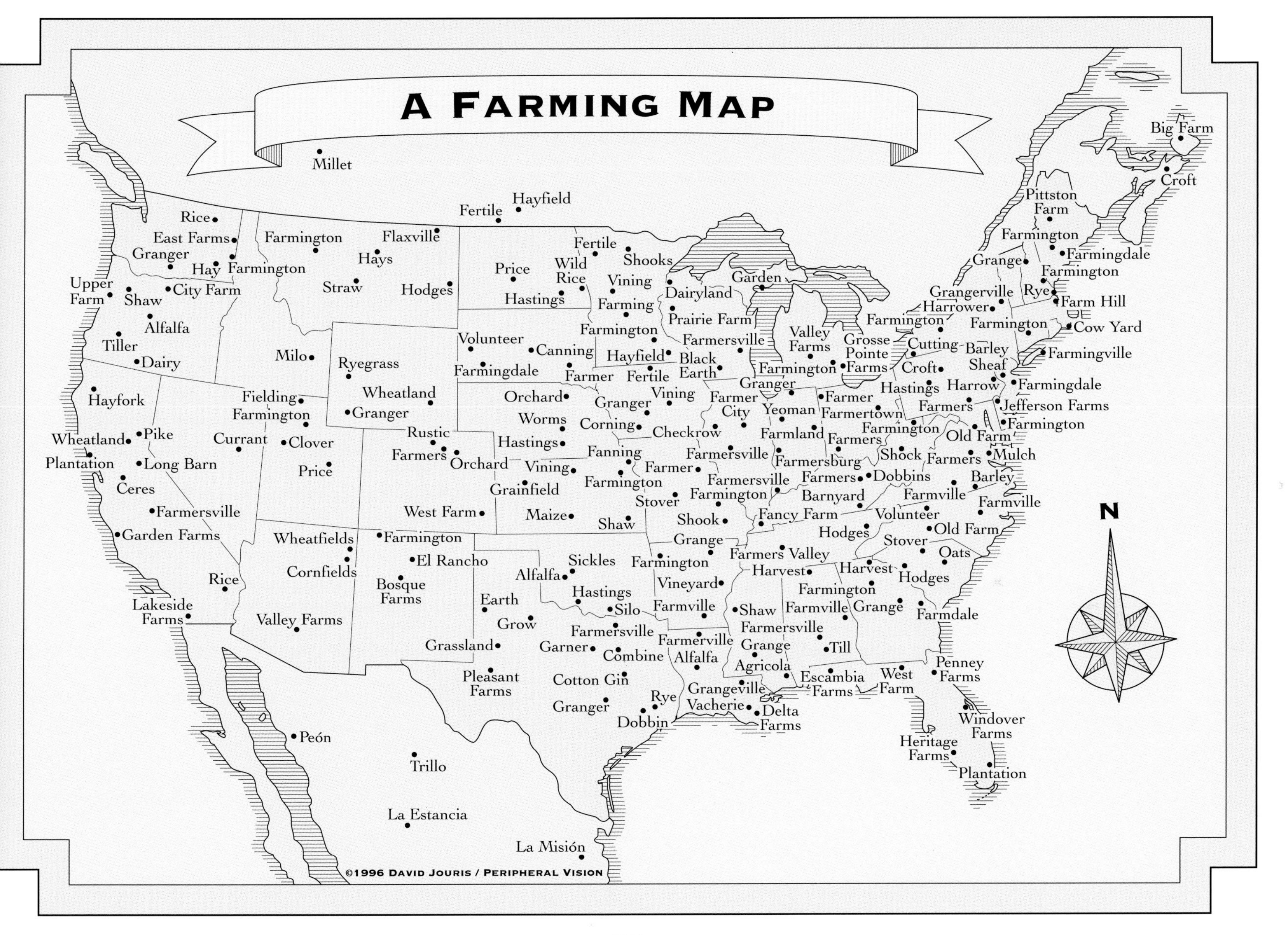
A FARMING MAP
Millet
Hayfield
Fertile
Rice
East Farms
Farmington
Flaxville
Granger
Hay
Farmington
Hays
Upper Farm
Shaw
City Farm
Straw
Hodges
Price
Alfalfa
Tiller
Dairy
Milo
Ryegrass
Hayfork
Fielding
Farmington
Wheatland
Granger
Wheatland
Pike
Currant
Clover
Plantation
Long Barn
Price
Ceres
Farmersville
Garden Farms
Rice
Lakeside Farms
Valley Farms
Wheatfields
Cornfields
Farmington
El Rancho
Bosque Farms
West Farm
Rustic
Farmers
Orchard
Grainfield
Maize
Volunteer
Farmingdale
Canning
Orchard
Worms
Hastings
Vining
Fertile
Wild Rice
Hastings
Shooks
Vining
Farming
Farmington
Hayfield
Farmer
Fertile
Granger
Corning
Fanning
Farmington
Stover
Shaw
Vining
Checkrow
Farmer
Dairyland
Prairie Farm
Farmersville
Black Earth
Garden
Farmer City
Farmersville
Farmersville
Farmington
Shook
Grange
Farmington
Sickles
Alfalfa
Hastings
Silo
Vineyard
Farmville
Earth
Grow
Grassland
Pleasant Farms
Farmersville
Garner
Combine
Cotton Gin
Granger
Rye
Dobbin
Farmerville
Alfalfa
Grangeville
Vacherie
Delta Farms
Agricola
Grange
Farmersville
Shaw
Farmers Valley
Harvest
Fancy Farm
Valley Farms
Farmington
Grosse Pointe Farms
Granger
Yeoman
Farmland
Farmersburg
Farmer
Farmertown
Farmers
Farmers
Barnyard
Dobbins
Hodges
Farmington
Harvest
Farmville
Grange
Till
Escambia Farms
West Farm
Penney Farms
Windover Farms
Heritage Farms
Plantation
Farmdale
Hodges
Oats
Stover
Old Farm
Volunteer
Farmville
Farmville
Barley
Shock
Farmers
Mulch
Farmington
Old Farm
Hastings
Farmers
Jefferson Farms
Farmington
Harrow
Farmingdale
Croft
Cutting
Barley
Sheaf
Farmington
Harrower
Grangerville
Farmington
Farmingville
Cow Yard
Farm Hill
Rye
Farmington
Grange
Farmingdale
Farmington
Pittston Farm
Croft
Big Farm
Peón
Trillo
La Estancia
La Misión
N
©1996 DAVID JOURIS / PERIPHERAL VISION

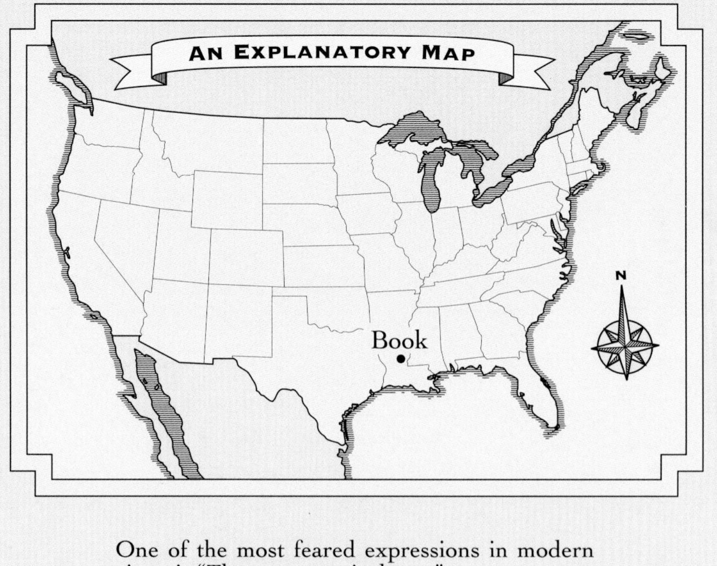

One of the most feared expressions in modern times is "The computer is down."
—NORMAN AUGUSTINE

COLOPHON

This atlas was designed and produced on an Apple Macintosh computer using the Aldus programs FreeHand and PageMaker. The typefaces are Cochin and Copperplate from Adobe Systems. A database of towns, from which the maps were made, was created using the program Microsoft Word. An Iomega Zip drive provided external storage and backup. A laser printer from GCC Technologies was used for proofing. And all of these items worked splendidly.

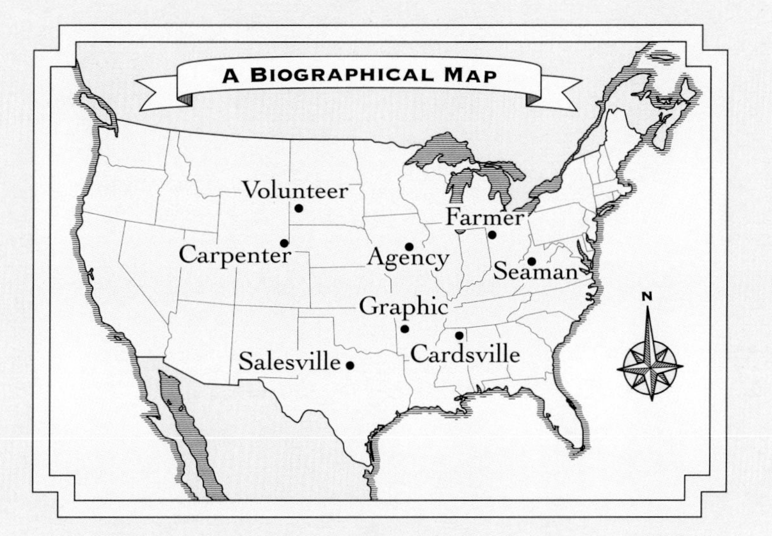

The only good reason for doing anything
is for fun.
—W. H. AUDEN

ABOUT THE AUTHOR

David Jouris has been a carpenter, farmer, and seaman. He has been employed by a video production company, clothing manufacturer, and greeting-card company. He has worked for an architect in Berlin, a travel agency in Ghent, and the United Nations in Aranyaprathet. He is a photographer, graphic artist, and mapmaker. This is his second atlas.

What to do next? It was a momentous question.
—Mark Twain

What's Ahead?

Already well underway is a thematic atlas of Western Europe featuring towns that actually exist. Among the maps nearing completion are confusion, English, reversibility, translation, misspelling, brevity, and (ever-popular) cheese.